P9-CIS-404

362.828   Edelman
E21f   Families in peril

GLENDALE COLLEGE LIBRARY

1500 N. VERDUGO RD.
GLENDALE, CA   91208

Families in Peril

The W. E. B. Du Bois Lectures   1986
Sponsored by the Ford Foundation

DISCARD

Families in Peril

AN AGENDA FOR SOCIAL CHANGE

MARIAN WRIGHT EDELMAN

Harvard University Press

Cambridge, Massachusetts, and London, England

362.828
E21f

Copyright © 1987 by the President and Fellows
  of Harvard College
All rights reserved
Printed in the United States of America
10 9 8 7 6 5 4 3 2

This book is printed on acid-free paper, and its binding
materials have been chosen for strength and durability.

Library of Congress Cataloging-in-Publication Data

Edelman, Marian Wright.
  Families in peril.

  (The W.E.B. Du Bois lectures; 1986)
  Includes index.
    1. Family policy—United States.   2. Afro-American
families.   3. Poor—United States.
4. Family—United States.   I. Title.   II. Series.
HV699.E34   1987   362.8′28′0973   86-29410
ISBN 0-674-29228-6 (alk. paper)

Designed by Gwen Frankfeldt

9/87

To three wonderful sons—
Joshua Robert,
Jonah Martin, and
Ezra Benjamin

Preface

I was honored to be asked to deliver the 1986 W. E. B. Du Bois
Lectures on which this book is based. One of Dr. Du Bois's *Pray-
ers for Dark People* (ed. Herbert Aptheker, Amherst, Mass.,
1981, p. 21) is my own for all of us today: "Give us grace, O God,
to do the deed which we well know cries to be done. Let us not
hesitate because of ease, or the words of men's mouths, or our
own lives. Mighty causes are calling us—the freeing of women,
the training of children, the putting down of hate and murder and
poverty—all these and more. But they call with voices that mean
work and sacrifice and death. Mercifully grant us, O God, the
spirit of Esther, that we say: I will go unto the King and if I perish,
I perish—Amen."

This book describes the overall and comparative status of black
and white children and families in America; the unacceptable human and public costs that result from widespread child and family
poverty; our nation's failure to invest adequately and preventively

in all our young—black and white, poor and middle class alike; the historical role of government in bolstering families—a tradition inadequately extended to our poorest and minority families; and the strong black tradition of self-help in a society unwilling to open doors for blacks as it did for others. I will explain why we need greater policy emphasis on preventing the poverty that makes children our poorest Americans and that threatens to produce what some label a permanent "underclass"; call for immediate, comprehensive national campaigns to prevent teenage pregnancy, infant mortality, and early childhood deprivation as a means of long-term deficit reduction as well as child-survival strategies; and outline the need for and ingredients of more effective leadership at all levels of American society if we are to redirect misguided national priorities and remove the economic and social barriers that cripple millions of children and families and rob America of vitally needed human resources for the twenty-first century.

At the outset I want to provide a context for my remarks. Although I am a doer rather than a scholar, I believe that effective action on any issue requires thorough fact-finding and analysis, a capacity to see a problem whole and then to break it into manageable pieces for action, to delineate clear long-term, intermediate, and short-term goals, and to pursue those goals through a range of strategies that must be constantly evaluated and adapted to changing political and community needs. I am less interested in formulating theoretical frameworks of policy for children and families than I am in feeding, clothing, healing, housing, and educating as many American children as soon as possible. In other words, I am more interested in helping families than in formulating something called family policy.

Labels as well as strategies and tactics change depending on the issue, the political atmosphere, the goal, the likely opportunities, and the allies needed to succeed on specific issues or to move ahead in behalf of poor children and families. I try to keep my eye on the child and on the specific need or set of needs I am trying to address. But, because fragmented and single-strategy responses to complex social problems often create as many problems as they solve, I try to see how the remedies to a specific need will add up over time to a coherent whole.

At the Children's Defense Fund (CDF), which I have been privileged to head since its inception, we are most interested in helping those children in American society who have the least. In order to do this, we try to articulate their needs in such a way that those who have more can be convinced that helping to ensure the economic well-being of others serves their own self-interest (either because they will feel good that they have done the right thing at a not-too-great cost or because they will realize that their own economic or social interest is also served).

We believe that the best way to help poor black children is to show that white children are similarly affected. CDF came into being in the early 1970s because we recognized that support for whatever was labeled black and poor was shrinking and that new ways had to be found to articulate and respond to the continuing problems of poverty and race, ways that appealed to the self-interest as well as the conscience of the American people. In each case, therefore, we ask how a particular condition affects all children and then examine how it differentially affects poor or minority or handicapped children. In designing remedies we also try to keep an eye on building the broadest possible constituency, while ensuring that the least privileged among our children are adequately protected.

I am a determined optimist. I believe the 1980s and 1990s are ripe for a positive change in our national commitment to poor children if thoughtful leadership can harness rising concern over pervasive child and family poverty.

The tide of misery that poverty breeds and that blacks have borne disproportionately throughout history has now spread to a critical mass of white American families and children. Thirty-three million—one-seventh of all Americans, including 13 million children—are now poor as a result of economic recession, structural changes in the economy, stagnated wages, federal tax and budget policies that favor the rich at the expense of the poor, and changing family demographics that result in one in every five American children living in a female-headed household, and one in four being dependent on welfare at some point in his or her lifetime.

The resultant rise in hunger, child and wife abuse, and homelessness has become a daily reality that has touched our lives either directly, through our neighbors or churches or synagogues, or indirectly, through our television screens. Not even President Reagan's politics of illusion can any longer hide the widespread suffering in our city streets and farmlands.

More Americans now personally know that poverty is not just the result of personal inadequacy, laziness, and unworthiness, despite our national leaders' attempts to portray the poor as culpable. Iowa farmers, Detroit autoworkers, Youngstown steelworkers, South Carolina textile-makers, and small business people, who have lost the shirts off their backs during the recession, now find themselves in food lines and full of despair. They thought it only happened to other people. After all, individuals in America are supposed to be self-sufficient, we have all been told, despite social and economic upheaval that renders obsolete many of the most willing workers.

More Americans are coming alive to the reality of how much worthier the poor must be than the rich to receive their national government's support. At a time when the wealthiest corporations received tax breaks that drained the national treasury of tens of billions annually, the much touted federal safety net left nearly three-quarters of the unemployed without unemployment insurance and 35 million Americans without public or private health insurance.

That more Americans are coming alive to these realities is seen in some progress made even since I delivered the Du Bois lectures and since the body of this book was revised for publication. Congress has passed and the President has signed the Tax Reform Act of 1986, which has as a centerpiece some real reform for low-income working families. As of 1988, poor families' federal taxes will generally be restored to 1979 levels or lower, reversing the nearly decade-long tax rise that has burdened the poor. Congress also rejected almost all of the President's proposed cuts for fiscal year 1987 in programs essential to poor children's health and well-being, and it forced the President to accept more than two billion dollars in program improvements for 1987. We thereby moved further along the path of restoring the drastic 1981 cuts and buttressing important programs that have proven positive effects. These are just first steps, however, and the problems described in this book are as present and real for America's poor as when the lectures were delivered.

Even the most callous conservatives are having second thoughts about continuing to blame poor children for their worsening mortality rates, hunger, homelessness, and abuse. But if any group is still blamed for its poverty, it is blacks, not whites, so that is where I will begin in Chapter 1.

In Chapter 2 I discuss white poverty and suggest a range of preventive investment strategies in health, nutrition, and child care to address the immediate survival needs of poor black and white children, as well as steps to raise the minimum wage, exempt the working poor from federal taxes, and bolster education and employment opportunities for black and white family heads.

In Chapter 3 I call for a comprehensive campaign to prevent teen pregnancy and share the range of measures we at CDF are taking to prevent the first teen birth and repeat teen births, and to ensure that all teen mothers receive comprehensive prenatal care, and stay in school. The core of CDF's teen pregnancy prevention effort is hope, which we believe is the best contraceptive. Hope must flow from rebuilding a framework of community values and support bolstered by private sector and government policies aimed at improving the self-esteem and life options for every child and youth.

Chapter 4 deals with welfare-reform strategies as one element in a larger self-sufficiency effort to prevent the poverty of female-headed households and the development of a so-called permanent underclass.

Finally I discuss how to get things done through more effective leadership by all elements of American society. For these complex black and white family problems can only be solved by the joint efforts of black and white community leaders, the private sector, and all levels of government. I am frankly tired of hearing people say that "only the black community can solve the black family issue," or that the private sector alone can meet all the needs of the homeless or unemployed, implying that government has no hand in creating any of the conditions against which families struggle.

This book, as all I do, draws on the efforts and research of many Children's Defense Fund staff members, to whom I am deeply grateful. Special thanks go to Paul Smith, Jim Weill, Barbara Savage, and Beverley Gallimore. I also want to thank Professor Nathan I. Huggins and his colleagues at the W. E. B. Du Bois Institute for their warm hospitality and assistance.

October 1986   M.W.E.

Contents

Families in Peril

There is only one sure basis of social reform
and that is Truth—a careful detailed knowledge of the essential facts of each social problem. Without this there is no logical starting
place for reform and uplift.

—W. E. Burghardt Du Bois
and Augustus Granville Dill,
The Negro Artisan

1 · The Black Family in America

After a period of not-so-benign neglect, the black family is back in
the public eye. The spiraling percentage of black female-headed
households and the problems associated with teenage pregnancies
have been graphically chronicled by Bill Moyers on CBS Reports'
"Vanishing Family," in *Ebony, Time,* and the *New Republic* cover
stories, and in a spate of front-page series in the *Washington Post*
and numerous local and national papers.

The attention of the media is a welcome development. Unless,
as so often happens, the glare of the spotlight leads us to despair
or to look for quick fixes and simplistic answers to complex family
problems that require long-term attention and multiple remedies.
Or unless proposed solutions are twisted into general attacks on
supposed failures in social programs or are transformed into a new
cycle of blaming the victim and greater race and class polarization.

A 1985 Children's Defense Fund (CDF) study, *Black and White
Children in America: Key Facts,* found that black children have

been sliding backward. Black children today are more likely to be born into poverty, lack early prenatal care, have a single mother or unemployed parent, be unemployed as teenagers, and not go to college after high school graduation than they were in 1980.

Compared to white children, we found that black children are

twice as likely to

· die in the first year of life
· be born prematurely
· suffer low birthweight
· have mothers who received late or no prenatal care
· see a parent die
· live in substandard housing
· be suspended from school or suffer corporal punishment
· be unemployed as teenagers
· have no parent employed
· live in institutions;

three times as likely to

· be poor
· have their mothers die in childbirth
· live with a parent who has separated
· live in a female-headed family
· be placed in an educable mentally retarded class
· be murdered between five and nine years of age
· be in foster care
· die of known child abuse;

four times as likely to

· live with neither parent and be supervised by a child welfare agency
· be murdered before one year of age or as a teenager

· be incarcerated between fifteen and nineteen years of age;

five times as likely to

·) be dependent on welfare; and

twelve times as likely to

· live with a parent who never married.

We also found that:

· Only four out of every ten black children, compared to eight out of every ten white children live in two-parent families.
· Births to unmarried teenagers occur five times more often among blacks than whites, although birth rates for black teens, married and unmarried, have been *declining,* while the birth rate among white unmarried teens has been *increasing* in recent years.
· In 1983, 58 percent of all births to black women were out of wedlock. Among black women under the age of twenty, the proportion was over 86 percent. For thirty years these out-of-wedlock ratios have increased inexorably. They have now reached levels that essentially guarantee the poverty of many black children for the unforeseeable future.

Whether black or white, young women under the age of twenty-five who head families with children are very likely to be poor. The poverty rates in 1983 were 85.2 percent for young black female-headed families and 72.1 percent for young white female-headed families. But black female-headed families are much more likely to stay poor. In female-headed families with older mothers, aged twenty-five to forty-four, there is a 20 percentage-point gap between black and white poverty rates.

Today black children in young female-headed households are the poorest in the nation. While a black child born in the United States has a one in two chance of being born poor, a black child in a female-headed household has a two in three chance of being poor. If that household is headed by a mother under twenty-five years of age, that baby has a four in five chance of being poor.

We all know that family income is usually lower if there is only one parent or if the parents are black. We often overlook the increasing importance of the parents' age in determining the family's income. For example, as the accompanying table shows, among female-headed families, those with young women as household heads are far more likely to be poor. The poverty rate among all families with heads under twenty-five (including those with two parents) is 29.4 percent, almost three times the national average; nearly as high as among all female-headed families (34.5 percent); and higher than among those families headed by a woman over forty-five.

Correlation between poverty rate and age of female heads of family.

Age	Poverty rate (percent)		
	White	Black	Total
Under 25	73.8	84.8	77.9
25–44	38.7	58.8	45.5
45–64	27.5	51.2	36.2

Black teens are having fewer rather than more babies: 172,000 births in 1970; 137,000 in 1983. The proportion of black women under twenty who have given birth has been falling steadily since the early 1970s and will probably reach the 1940s level before the end of the decade. However, the percentage of those births that were to unmarried teens soared 50 percent—from 36 percent in 1950 to 86 percent by 1981. Among black women reaching their twentieth birthday between 1945 and 1949, 40 percent had given birth. Among black women reaching their twentieth birthday between 1975 and 1979, 44 percent had given birth—an increase of only 4 percent. From 1947 to 1977, however, the marriage rate for pregnant black fifteen- to seventeen-year-olds dropped about 80 percent; and for black eighteen- and nineteen-year-olds the marriage rate is down about 60 percent.

Today's young white population also is less likely to let pregnancy lead to marriage, but the decline is nowhere near as great. Seven percent of white teen births were out of wedlock in 1960,

17 percent in 1970, and 39 percent in 1983. Among pregnant white fifteen- to seventeen-year-olds, the proportion marrying before birth fell from 62 to 43 percent during the same thirty year period (1947 to 1977), while the proportion of pregnant eighteen- and nineteen-year-olds who married fell from 52 to 50 percent. The current white prenatal marriage rates are still much higher than the corresponding black rates were even back in 1950. Such changes in marriage rates have a dramatic effect on determining the proportion of all births that are to unmarried mothers. Every prenatal marriage in effect counts twice: by removing a birth to an unmarried mother, and by adding a birth to a married one.

It is important to identify why the proportion of out-of-wedlock teen births is rising. The cause among black teenagers is a drop in marriage rates, not an increase in birth rates. Among white teens the cause is more babies coupled with a decrease in marriage among those who become pregnant.

In 1970 teens accounted for half of all out-of-wedlock births. In 1983 almost two-thirds of the babies born to unmarried women were to women twenty and over. This is true for whites and blacks (63.4 percent white; 63.0 percent black). Again, while the share of out-of-wedlock births occurring to adult women has been going up for both blacks and whites, the reasons for the increase are different. Birth rates for white unmarried women (aged sixteen to forty-four) have been going up (19.3 per 1,000 in 1983) because more unmarried white adult women are having babies. Birth rates for unmarried black women have been going down (95.5 per 1,000 in 1970; 77.7 in 1983), but fewer young black women are getting married, and married black women are having fewer babies. (In 1984 there were 89.1 births per 1,000 white married women aged eighteen to forty-four; there were 79.3 births per 1,000 black married women. In 1984, 65 percent of all white women but only 43 percent of all black women were married.)

In 1980 pregnant *married* black women were two and one-half times as likely to have an abortion as pregnant married white women.[1] Having a child can mean a substantial loss of family income to a married black woman. Among two-parent families with incomes over $25,000, 83 percent of black women work, compared to 62 percent of white women.[2] And the black woman's salary contributes a bigger share of total family income than does the white woman's. For many married black women, an additional child may tip the scales back toward economic insecurity.

The crux of the problem facing the black family today is that young black women who become pregnant do not marry nearly as often as they used to. Nor as often as young pregnant white women do. Why young black marriages do not form is thus central to our concern about the proportion of black children in female-headed families. That is especially true since the *whole* of the increase in the proportion of black children in female-headed families over the last decade is accounted for by the increase in those who live with unmarried mothers, and not by the increase in the proportion who live with divorced or separated mothers.

In 1981, among the infants born to fifteen- to seventeen-year-olds, 48 percent of those born to white teenagers were out-of-wedlock, compared to 94 percent of those born to black teenagers. CDF research staff used data to determine what would happen if black teen girls had behaved as white teen girls had. In general the white young women were less likely to be sexually active, more likely to abort if they did become pregnant, and more likely to marry before birth if they decided to carry the child to term. We can project what would have happened if young black women had matched each white rate.

If black teens had been no more sexually active than white teens, the proportion of births to black unmarried mothers would only have fallen from 94 to 93 percent. Similarly negligible results held for applying white contraceptive efficiency or white abortion rates. But if the black young women had adopted white prenatal marriage rates, the out-of-wedlock ratio would have fallen to only 56 percent, not very far above the actual white rate of 48 percent.

Some Scholarly Perspectives on the Black Family

Before analyzing the complex economic and social factors that have led to 58 percent of black babies today being born to single mothers, it is important to remind ourselves that the stereotype is just that—a stereotype—true in too many cases but not others: millions of black families are not on welfare, have children who stay in school, stay out of trouble, and do not get pregnant, and, if they fall on hard times, find a way to overcome. Many single mothers are doing a valiant job which we should affirm and learn from. Until recently, two-parent families have been the black family norm, despite great publicity given to black female-headed families. It is only in the 1980s that the majority of black infants have been born to unmarried mothers—the culmination of a trend that began in the 1950s. However, since black families began to be studied from the turn of the twentieth century, black and white scholars alike have been concerned with out-of-wedlock births and single-parenting.

In their concern over the effects of slavery, urbanization, and unemployment on black families, a number of scholars have identified female-headed households or matriarchy as the characteristic and pathological element making and keeping black families "inferior" to white families. Until the 1960s many analysts assumed that there was something wrong with the black family, which was described at best as nonfunctional and disorganized.

In the last twenty years other researchers have begun to look at black families a bit differently and to emphasize their strengths; to try to distinguish between myths, stereotypes, and facts; to identify African retentions that may make black families different from but equally as functional as white families; and to look at the effects of social and economic inequalities and discrimination. These more recent scholars insist that past research suffered from stereotypical historical and sociological judgments and poor empirical methodology. Slavery was assumed to have left American blacks with little culture and no behavioral norms; thus, acculturation of white norms was shoddy and slow. Early researchers blamed black poverty and disorganization on the failure to establish strong marital bonds.

A variety of researchers have used various terms to categorize the differing perspectives on the black family. Those perspectives fall essentially into three groups, according to the way scholars thought black families functioned and the cause(s). I will call the dominant early perspective the *cultural deficiency* view. Black families were seen as different from and unequal to white families, especially white middle-class families, which were the norm used. Most black families were characterized by instability, suffering not only from economic troubles and discrimination but also from promiscuity and matriarchy. Some critics went as far as to suggest pathology in black family functioning. The causes for all this were slavery (the splitting up of families, emasculation of the black male, lack of cultural tradition) and urbanization (the lack of community and behavioral norms, splitting up of families, unemployment). Proponents of this viewpoint, however, did not all agree on how blacks could be helped and whether black families could ever become more like white ones. They did all tend to see black families as homogeneous and in trouble.[3]

The next perspective, the *cultural variance* view, developed as a response to the first. The scholars holding it considered black and white culture as different but equal and therefore felt that the black family had to be judged according to its own culture and values. These differences had developed because black Americans did retain African mores and behavior norms; therefore a distinct Afro-American subculture has emerged. According to this perspective, blacks, because of our history in the United States, have had to adapt differently and develop different family structures from whites. However, these structures are as functional for blacks as white structures are for whites. Instead of making judgments about inferiority and pathology, society needs to recognize that blacks function under a different value system and socialization process.[4]

Some researchers who might fit into this category assert that African retentions have contributed significantly to Black American culture and that we need to look at ways that black families have functioned positively and have survived over the years (without necessarily comparing them to white families). Yet they may not actually agree that blacks function under a totally separate value system from the rest of society. Another group concentrates more on similarities between black and white families than on differences. We might add a subcategory for them, calling it cultural *equivalency*. It accounts for those scholars—mostly historians—who find that, throughout history, black Americans have formed two-parent families, have maintained intact families, and have family structures and functioning similar if not identical to whites. Thus, they reject talk about a separate or inferior culture and different black family functioning.[5]

Another major outlook on black families can be called the *social class* view, which assumes that if blacks were not so poor and did not suffer from racism and discrimination, their families would be much like white families. The problem is that economic inequities have left the majority of the black population in the lower income class. Poverty and lack of opportunities have destabilized and handicapped black families. They are not, however, inherently different or inferior to white families. Given equal opportunities and compensation for past inequities, black families would be no different from white ones.[6]

The 1980s finds more scholars attempting to take a new look at black families, to reconcile the conflicting views and research, to develop a new methodology based on a cultural understanding of black families and accurate empirical information, to leave behind the stereotypes and misunderstandings of the past, and to look at black families as heterogenous and functional, as resulting from both African and American traditions, and as exemplary of both weaknesses and strengths.[7]

I am not going to spend time arguing about differing scholarly views. Nor am I able to resolve whether it is the change in black family structure which causes its desperate economic condition or family destabilizing changes in the economy which have led to black family changes. I believe that poor female-headed households, male joblessness, and poverty are all parts of the same conundrum which we must act to pierce now, rather than just continue to debate whether the chicken or the egg came first.

Certainly we need to understand as much as we can, and thoughtful academic research and exchange on cause and effect are needed. But we cannot afford to wait for a precise disaggregation before we act to save another generation of black young.

Where Are the Black Fathers?

Since the main reason that black children live with only a mother is that most unmarried pregnant black women do not marry before giving birth, what has become of the fathers? They remain single. The pattern is quite clear.

According to United States Census reports 27.3 percent of white males aged twenty to twenty-four have married; only 11.9 percent of black males of the same age have married. Among white males aged twenty-five to twenty-nine, 64.9 percent have married; among black males of the same age, only 44.3 percent have married.[8]

If black marital rates for males in their twenties equaled those of white males in that age group, there would be an additional 450,000 married black males. That should be compared to about 750,000 black female-headed families with children where the female head is also under thirty years of age.

If marriage rates were the same, not every one of these men would marry one of these unmarried mothers. Yet any reasonable set of assumptions will show that an increase in the marital rate among young black men to the white level would reduce the proportion of fatherless young black families by between one-half and two-thirds. Thus, the failure of first marriages to form among young blacks is the largest single cause of the very high proportion of all young black families that are fatherless.

It is not the only cause, so I will mention other less important, but real, causes.

First, historically young black males have always been institutionalized—primarily imprisoned—at rates much higher than those of white males. In 1980, 5 percent of black men versus 1 percent of white men in their twenties were institutionalized. But this excess incarceration rate would, if eliminated, supply at most about 40,000 newly married men (even assuming that they were all single and that they all married at white rates). That is less than one-tenth the number to be found if the noninstitutionalized young black men were as likely as whites to marry.

Second, young black men are more than twice as likely to be in the military and living in barracks as are young white men. However, this disparity could supply fewer than 20,000 additional fathers. And, interestingly in light of what I will discuss later, the racial difference in marital status disappears for young men in the military. Obviously young men in military service are less likely to be married than civilians of the same age for all races; but almost 18 percent of the white, and over 20 percent of the black males in the military are married.

Third, black males are far more likely to marry nonblack females than black females are to marry nonblack males. But the numbers are small in either case.

Fourth, black males die at nearly twice the white rates. Among males in their twenties this is primarily because of the excess of deaths by homicide among black males. Among twenty-year-old men, 3.3 percent of the black males and 1.8 percent of the white males will die before reaching the age of thirty. It is urgent that this disparity be reduced quickly in order to recover these wasted lives. Even so, we will not thereby regain more than a percent or so of the missing young black fathers.

The last factor we must take into account is the most difficult to document: those young black males who are missing from the Census. The extent of the undercount of young black males is necessarily speculative. A few black males can be shown to be missing among the eighteen- and nineteen-year-olds. But among those twenty and over, the numbers are substantial by even the most conservative count. The Children's Defense Fund (CDF) estimates that a minimum of 8.1 percent, or about 210,000, black men in their twenties are missing from the census.

These young black men are those who are most often pointed to as members of an underground economy, or as "hidden" within households headed by black women who receive public aid. The reality is more complex. In one simple sense, we know that they are in an underground economy. They don't die, so they must eat. That need not imply a criminal source of support. Men who hide from creditors, including collectors of child-support payments, do so primarily because they have aboveground income they seek to retain. Still, let us suppose them criminals concealing their incomes and themselves from the census-taker. Are they currently adequate, although undetected, fathers for black children? I think not. Criminal earnings average very little and incur great risk when pursued over any substantial number of years; and it takes almost twenty years to raise a child.

Moreover, black males who are criminals do not do well. White-collar crimes are the profitable ones. The data suggest that the missing black males are even less well-educated than those we record and so are poorly placed to work the richest and safest criminal fields. The remaining violent and heinous crimes—robbery, burglary, drug-dealing, and pimping—are not a strong basis for a parent to provide adequately for a child.

The other alternative is that the missing young black males are hidden among the recipients of public assistance. Surely there are some. In almost half our states, an unemployed father must leave the home before the children are eligible for Aid for Families with Dependent Children (AFDC), no matter how low the family's income.

No doubt, not all impoverished fathers strictly abide by such welfare policies. A small minority probably survive in part off the AFDC benefits of their wives or girlfriends. However, if this failure of design in our AFDC program is the cause of a substantial number of the "missing" young black males, especially in states that do not provide assistance to intact families, it will be removed as soon as the program mandates coverage of intact families with unemployed workers.

The proportion of young black families with fathers fell drastically from 1970 to 1980. If the "missing black males" from the U.S. Census are centrally connected to this phenomenon of single-parent-family growth, then the proportion of all young black males who are missing ought to have increased equally drastically between the Census of 1970 and the Census of 1980.[9] Instead, that proportion has been constant. There is no reason to believe that they are the driving force behind the failure of new black two-parent families to form.

What does explain the 200,000 or so young black males who do not appear in national counts? Because of the variety of human existence, there are going to be a few men who fit every description I have mentioned. But I believe the majority are unemployable, disheartened, and derive little if any criminal income. As a matter of public policy, the nation has much to gain by reducing the number of black males who are of little value to the economy, even the criminal economy. The United Negro College Fund slogan is right: "A mind is a terrible thing to waste." How much greater is the loss when we discard the whole person of 200,000 black males.

Let us go back to the 450,000 black males who would be married if black marriage rates equaled white rates for men in their twenties. Because the real explanation lies not in finding the 200,000 missing men, but understanding the single status of this larger group. One crucial question is: When did the rate of marriage formation drop among young black males? In the 1970s it paralleled the decline of employment prospects of young black males, which resulted in only 29.8 percent of black teens and 61 percent of black twenty- to twenty-four-year-old men being employed by 1978.

From 1978 to 1985 things got a bit worse for both black teens and males in their twenties. The year 1986 was the first year in the history of the United States when the average number of black women who are employed exceeded the average number of black men who are employed. In 1985 there were only 39,000 more black male than black female workers. But there were over 12 million more white male than white female workers.

The black teen employment collapse during the 1960s and the employment collapse for blacks in their early twenties during the 1970s portend, distressingly, a currently occurring but not yet clearly quantified collapse in the employment situation of black males in their late twenties and thirties. The way this disaster has rolled up the age spectrum in the black community suggests that we must focus more of our efforts (though certainly not all) on teens—through education, job training, health care, and other services—and even on young children to prevent the repetition of this damage. (I frankly don't know how to get Bill Moyers' thirty-year-old Timothy into the mainstream job market at this point, although we must try. I do believe we must focus more resources on helping to prevent boys of twelve, thirteen, and fifteen, and their younger siblings, from becoming twenty-five or thirty-year-old dependent men.)

There is more than a correlation between declining black male employment and declining marriage rates among young blacks. There is cause and effect. When a pregnant single woman is resolved to bear the child, marriage is most likely under active consideration. If the father of the child, presumably a few years older than herself, is potentially a good provider, marriage may well result. But if the proportion of young males who are potentially good providers falls, we would expect to see the prenatal marriage rate decline. We have. Indeed, we would expect two substantial changes in young women's behavior to follow a decline in the "marriageability" of young males. First, fewer single women would become pregnant with a child that they planned to bear. Second, fewer pregnant single women, intent on bearing their child, would marry before giving birth. Those are exactly the two patterns we do find among young black women today.

My basic conclusion is that the key to bolstering black families, alleviating the growth in female-headed households, and reducing black child poverty lies in improved education, training, and employment opportunities for black males and females. (This must be coupled with a community support and value system that prepares young people for work that decent public policies must undergird. A strong community work ethic in the absence of work and training opportunities adds up to frustration and hopelessness.) This view is shared by many analysts of black family and civil rights organizations. William Wilson of the Department of Sociology at the University of Chicago says: "both the black delay in marriage and the lower rate of remarriage, each of which is associated with high percentages of out-of-wedlock births and female-headed households, can be directly tied to the labor market status of black males . . . We were able to document empirically that black women, especially young black women, are facing a shrinking pool of marriageable (that is, employed, economically stable) men."[10] The problem of black joblessness, Wilson argues, should once

working in cities around the country. Byllye Avery's National Black Women's Health Project, headquartered in Atlanta, has developed a national forum and supportive atmosphere for poor black women to come together to define and respond to their own health needs. Avery's self-help network and Daphne Busby's Sisterhood of Black Single Mothers in Brooklyn, New York, are tapping and affirming the enormous strengths of poor black women and communities and helping them organize to ensure their own individual and family well-being; to protect themselves and their children against the physical and emotional abuse of their internal and external worlds; and to protect their families and children against teen pregnancy and other self-limiting activities. The Shiloh Baptist Church in the inner city of Washington, D.C.—my church—has reinforced its deep-rooted commitment to strong family values by building, without outside help, a five-million-dollar Family Life Center. Scholarships, counseling, and tutoring for young people, day care, family recreation, and a range of other family-centered services and activities are as important a part of its ministry as Sunday-morning services. Numerous black churches are conducting similar education, day care, and senior-citizen activities.

This kind of individual, community, and religious group outreach and direct service self-help is being complemented by and hooked up with another kind of black leadership that is emerging from thoughtful black professionals who have committed themselves to strengthening disadvantaged children and families. Dr. Robert Johnson, director of Adolescent Medicine at the University of Medicine and Dentistry of New Jersey, in Newark, is working effectively with poor black adolescents to help them delay too-early sexual activity and pregnancy. Dr. Aaron Shirley has started three comprehensive school-based clinics in Jackson and other Mississippi communities. Dr. Bailus Walker, Massachusetts Health Commissioner, has systematically developed and implemented policies to lower infant mortality and improve the health status of poor children, black and white. They, in turn, are connecting up with the growing number of black social-services, welfare, child-welfare, and child-care officials and advocates around the country for the needed interdisciplinary and comprehensive approach to complex family problems. Collaboration and comprehensiveness are becoming the cornerstones of emerging teen pregnancy prevention and family strengthening efforts, as has an emphasis on building self-sufficiency. More people are recognizing that the traditional fragmented policy and service approach cannot solve social problems that are cumulative and complex. They also recognize that government effort without community awareness and support will not be enough.

These professionals are reaching out to work with the growing network of black elected officials like Jesse Oliver, a Texas state legislator, who, in 1985, skillfully shepherded through his legislature a $200 million indigent health care package. When fully implemented, it will benefit over 300,000 poor Texas mothers and children. Oliver is one of a growing group of state and local black political leaders mobilizing to use the political process to help black and white children and families in a tough-minded and effective manner.

Effective change strategies today involve the dull, technical details of policy and budget development. The absence of a single overriding national symbol like Dr. Martin Luther King, Jr. must not obscure the valiant and multiple efforts we are finding in black communities across the country that are beginning to rally together to recapture our youth and families.

This surge of black community energy and commitment is essential because we will have to reach many of our vulnerable children, teens, and parents on a one-to-one basis. It is also essential because the black community knows far better than anyone else—knows in its bones and in the hard school of experience—that without its own strong leadership now, as in the past, too little can be expected from government or other institutions. No one is more aware of the folly of relying solely on government to solve black community problems than the black community. The black American journey is one of making a way out of no way because we often had no one, save God, to lend us a hand. For most of our American sojourn, government has been opponent and victimizer rather than ally. Slavery and legally sanctioned segregation left to us the major burden of seeking our own freedom, protecting our own families, creating our own churches in which to worship, forming our own benevolent societies to bury our dead, developing our own home health remedies and hospitals to care for our sick, and opening up our homes and churches to teach our own children.

Federal affirmative-action strategies, under so much attack in the Reagan era, are a blip, like the singular precedent of Reconstruction in a long American history of affirmative action against blacks of indescribably greater magnitude. Increasingly we hear political "leaders" and read columnists who state or imply that the black community is asking government in the 1980s to assume responsibility for problems the black community brought upon itself and could and should solve itself, or that blacks are asking government for help different from or greater than that historically and currently provided other groups in the society.

Such politicians and journalists need to be reminded that we seek no more or less than what government has been willing, often eager, to do for others. They need to be reminded that the black community has always and will always do its utmost to solve its problems.

- Harriet Tubman did not wait for government to free the slaves. She made repeated journeys on her underground railroad into the Deep South to spirit out hundreds of slaves to freedom in the North.[11]

- Nat Turner and Denmark Vesey revolted against slavery and paid with their lives.

- Sojourner Truth and Frederick Douglass used their eloquence to speak out against and resist slavery, despite beatings and threats.

- Prince Hall founded one of the oldest social organizations among Negroes in America when, on March 6, 1775, he and fourteen other Negroes chartered a Lodge of Freemasons at Boston Harbor, which mushroomed into the hundreds of Masonic lodges throughout the United States today. As early as 1776 he urged the Massachusetts legislature to support emancipation and in 1797 prodded the city of Boston to provide schools for free Negro children. Before they eventually agreed to do so, he ran a school for black children in his own house, as did many other blacks.[12]

· The unwelcoming attitudes of white churches led Thomas Peel to organize independent Baptist churches, including congregations of Free Negroes in Boston and Philadelphia, and Richard Allen to found the African Methodist Episcopal Church.[13]

· Black journalists excluded from white newspapers started their own, for example, Monroe Trotter's *Boston Guardian*.[14]

· Ida Wells was one of many blacks who led the crusade against lynching.[15]

· A. Phillip Randolph organized the Brotherhood of Sleeping Car Porters in 1925 and fought racial discrimination within the labor unions all his life. He organized the celebrated March on Washington Movement during World War II—a precursor to the famous 1963 March—to prod the U.S. government into halting discrimination in industries having government contracts, the standards and enforcement of which we are still fighting for today.[16]

· Mary McLeod Bethune started Bethune Cookman College on a dump heap, with a ton of faith and a $5.00 down payment on a $250.00 note she and students worked to pay off.[17] She also founded the National Council of Negro Women, which Dorothy Height now heads and which is a leader in the struggle to strengthen black families today.

· Charles Houston, a black Harvard law school graduate, conceptualized and implemented the legal strategy that undermined legal segregation in the United States. He and a small band of lawyers, which included Thurgood Marshall and James Nabrit, and handfuls of brave black parents, knew they could not depend on the government to ensure fair treatment for black Americans when it was government that segregated them.[18]

· W. E. B. Du Bois spent a lifetime documenting, publicizing, and fighting discrimination against black Americans. Few, if any, ever approached his leadership in helping America become a more just society.

· And no American since Lincoln has aroused the conscience of the nation more than Martin Luther King, Jr.

But as important as black self-help is, and must continue to be, it is not enough. Teenage pregnancy and parenthood and the growth of female-headed households are intimately intertwined with poverty and lack of economic opportunity which flow from governmental policies or abdication of responsibility for some of its citizens. Changes in the economy have, over the past thirty years, undermined the capacity of black men to marry and support viable families. Short-lived or underfunded efforts to help poor families and children achieve self-sufficiency coupled with government policies that encouraged family breakup have hampered solutions to family problems. These lie at the heart of the black family crisis today.

A few cautions are in order because we are confronting a black and white family crisis that we must not lose and must not mess up by careless rhetoric, political posturing, or media-seeking. Preventing teen pregnancy and black family instability will require the greatest care, effort, and sensitivity on everyone's part, black and white, public and private. Who says what and how it is said will make an enormous difference in whether we see positive solutions or a polarized atmosphere. These complex problems will not be solved just by the media or by speeches. They can be derailed by the media or by speeches if we are not all careful in weighing what we say and how we say it, and if the media and political leaders cannot take the time and make the effort to learn about and present complex problems in more thorough ways.

It is critically important that we maintain an appropriately balanced view about who are the poor, both in our definition of the problem and in our consideration of proposed remedies. These remedies must go far beyond needed welfare reform. They must be more than mere moralizing.

In 1967, in *Where Do We Go From Here: Chaos or Community?* Martin Luther King, Jr., reflected on the renewed focus on the black family and cautioned: "As public awareness of the predicament of the Negro family increases, there will be danger and opportunity. The opportunity will be to deal fully rather than haphazardly with the problem of a whole—to see it as a social catastrophe . . . brought on by long years of brutality and oppression—and to meet it as other disasters are met, with an adequacy of resources. The danger will be that the problems will be attributed to innate Negro weaknesses and used to justify further neglect and to rationalize continued oppression."[19] Today, as the debate about the black family crisis is renewed, Dr. King's caution of two decades ago has tremendous vitality.

For God's sake and our children's future, let us seize the opportunities and avoid the dangers that we know are lurking. Let us focus on what unites us, on the overwhelming majority of poverty that we can do something about now, and on preventing another generation of black babies from becoming the poor black mothers and fathers that we so begrudgingly try to help today through our social policies.

There is no finer investment for
any community than putting milk
into babies.

—Sir Winston Churchill,
March 21, 1943

2 · The American Family in the 1980s

The American family crisis is not just a black family crisis. Both public and private sector neglect and anti-family policy have contributed to a downward spiral for families and children, black and white. Those who suffer the most are of course the poor. Although the data on poverty, family dissolution, and teenage pregnancy are grimmer for blacks than for whites, the data for whites and for our society as a whole are themselves quite grim. In some respects (education, income of two-parent families, women's earnings, child nutrition, infant mortality) black rates have been improving and narrowing the gap between whites—or were doing so until the budget cuts and near-depression of the early 1980s. In certain other respects the gap has been narrowing because blacks have been standing still while whites are slipping backward.

From 1969 to 1984 America's black child poverty rate went up one-sixth, but the white rate went up two-thirds. Given the huge disparity at the beginning point—the black rate was four times the white rate in 1969—we still have a far higher black child poverty rate, although it is now less than three times the white rate. Whites had far more ground to lose; and they have lost a lot of ground. In some respects this tells more about the economics and politics of the 1970s and 1980s than looking only at black rates.

The wage situation for young working-class whites is worse today than it was for young blacks in 1979. CDF recently obtained unpublished government data on the pay rates of the more than 50 million Americans paid on an hourly basis, and looked at who is paid at an hourly rate less than what is needed to keep a family out of poverty if the job is full-time. The proportion of workers of all ages making such inadequate wages nearly doubled from 1979 to 1984. And, while in both 1979 and 1984 the overall black rate was significantly higher than the white rate, between 1979 and 1984 the rate for young whites soared so much that it became substantially worse than the rate for young blacks was in 1979.

The change in out-of-wedlock teen birth rates tells a similar, albeit more complex story. The birth rate for unmarried black teens is going down, although it remains much higher than that of white teens. (In 1970 there were 96.9 births per thousand unmarried black women aged fifteen to nineteen; in 1980 the figure dropped to 89.2, and in 1983 to 86.4.) On the other hand, for unmarried white teens, birth rates increased by more than two-thirds from 1970 to 1983. (In 1970 there were 10.0 births per thousand unmarried white women aged fifteen to nineteen; in 1983 the figure was 18.5—an increase of 85 percent.)

These data tell us that in some respects the white family crisis has been growing while the black family crisis has stabilized or grown more slowly. In fact the proportion of all American families with children that were headed by women was, in 1985, equal to the proportion Daniel Patrick Moynihan identified as the essence of the crisis of the black family in his 1965 report. Some 21 percent of *all* families with children are now headed by a woman, just as was true of nonwhite families in the Census of 1960, Senator Moynihan's source.

This is not to say of course that American whites are worse off than blacks. But it is to say that, in some important respects, trends for blacks foreshadow trends for whites, or are exaggerated representations of broader problems in our society, as blacks are often hurt earlier and more profoundly by social or economic changes that injure all poor and working-class Americans. What we see and hear, what we read in the media, what political leaders say when they talk about teen pregnancy or child poverty or the underclass, is often directed at blacks. If not so directed, it is often construed by the majority of Americans as pertaining only to blacks. Actually the phenomena are far more complex.

The political relationship between blacks as a disproportionately poor group and American attitudes toward and treatment of poor people in general is extraordinarily complex. Does the fact that blacks are disproportionately poor in a country with a history of legalized racial segregation make it harder for the society to come to grips with broader poverty? Or does the premium that Americans put on economic success and the stigma applied to the lack of such success deepen negative attitudes toward blacks because they have been disproportionately poor? Almost certainly the answer to *both* questions is yes. This kind of "chicken-and-egg" problem is beyond the scope of this book. I would rather concentrate on how to get out of the bind, how to get Americans to recognize that poverty is far from being a black problem per se, that success or the absence of it is dictated for many—black and white—by social policy, and that we have a tremendous mutuality of interest in redressing the causes and effects of poverty and family break-up for all Americans.

American Children in Poverty

First we must recognize that, if only by dint of their overwhelmingly majority status, whites make up most of the children and young adults about whom we should be concerned.

· Nearly half of all black children in the United States are poor, an appalling figure. But a sixth of white children are poor, and that is also appalling. There are 8.1 million poor *white* children in the

U.S., and 4.3 million poor black children—a two to one ratio. Together, more than one out of five American children are poor, including nearly one out of four children under the age of six.

The poverty line is an income level that the federal government sets to approximate the amount of money that will allow a frugal family to pay for its most essential needs. It varies by family size. In 1984, for example, the poverty line was $10,609 for a family of four and $8,277 for a family of three.

Overall, children in America have become far poorer than other age groups. During the past fifteen years their poverty rates have soared, even as poverty among adults generally has stayed stable.

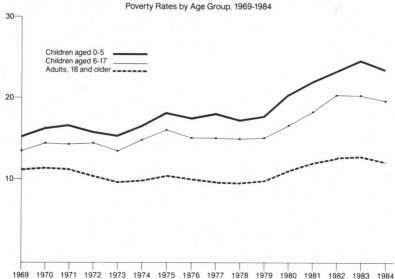

Poverty Rates by Age Group, 1969-1984

Children aged 0-5
Children aged 6-17
Adults, 18 and older

1969 1970 1971 1972 1973 1974 1975 1976 1977 1978 1979 1980 1981 1982 1983 1984

Source: *A Children's Defense Budget: An Analysis of the FY 1987 Federal Budget and Children* (Washington, D.C.: Children's Defense Fund, 1986), p. 8.

Not only have the numbers of children in poverty increased since 1979, but poor families have become poorer while rich families have become richer. In 1983 more than 42 percent of the 13 million poor children lived in families with incomes below 50 percent of the poverty line ($3,969 for a family of three and $5,089 for a family of four), while the top 10 percent of families averaged $5,000 or more income (after inflation) in 1984 than in 1980.

Nor has the economic "recovery" done much to mitigate the recent surge in child poverty. Only 210,000 children were lifted out of poverty in 1983 and 1984, two years of economic recovery, and a fraction of the 3,146,000 children—75 percent of them white—who had fallen into poverty from 1979 to 1982. The child poverty rate is still higher than at any time since the early 1960s. At the rate of improvement that took place in 1983 and 1984, and assuming we suffer no more recessions, it would take thirty years—nearly two generations—to get the number of poor children back to the 1979 level, which even then was intolerable.

In other respects as well, the family crisis involves more white than black children.

- Black teen birth rates are higher than white rates, but 69 percent of teen births in America are to whites.
- A higher proportion of black children live in single-parent families; overall, however, 9 million white children live with a single parent, as 5 million black children do.

By these and other criteria that we identify as part of the crises of poverty and family, the problems transcend racial lines. All children—whether white, black, or brown; Native American or Asian; male or female; urban or rural—have one thing in common; it is their most important characteristic. It is that they are children and must depend on adults to help them. The question we must confront is the extent to which children can depend on us, and how we organize our society, our government, to help meet children's needs. This question must be considered in contexts that demolish the perception that most of the children needing and getting our help are poor and black. One such context is the white child poverty and family crisis I have just described. Another is understanding how the government is helping all families, poor and non-poor. And a third is understanding how throughout the history of the United States we have given assistance to families, overwhelmingly white, to help them meet the needs of their children.

One such child was born in Fort Benning, Georgia, in 1942, where his father was living on a federal veterans disability pension.

He attended the University of Georgia, a public university, where his tuition and expenses were paid by the federal War Orphans Act. He had planned to go into physics; but learning that physics postdoctoral fellows got low pay, he did graduate work in economics, paid for by a federal National Defense Education Act fellowship. He started his career teaching at Texas A & M, a federal land-grant college.

This is a success story: how specific federal programs at their best help a child attain self-sufficiency. That child is now a United States Senator. His name is Phil Gramm.[1] He is a conservative who essentially would do away with federal help for children today. In 1981 he was one of the prime authors of the law that cut benefits drastically in virtually every federal program for low-income children—a law referred to as Gramm-Latta. He shares some of the responsibility for the loss of federal aid to 90,000 students in higher education. And he is one of the prime authors of the Gramm-Rudman-Hollings balanced budget amendment, which threatens to wreak even greater havoc on federal programs for needy children and families.

I do not know Senator Gramm. But he seems to suffer from a peculiarly American amnesia that wants us to believe families are wholly self-sufficient; that makes us forget how government helped all of us when we were children, and helps all of us as adults; and that makes us believe that the government is simply wasting its billions on a wholly dependent, self-perpetuating class of poor people, while doing nothing but taxing the rest of us.

These beliefs—about which children and families government has traditionally helped and how and why—serve as a backdrop for examining appropriate public and private roles and responsibilities in ensuring that we meet the survival needs and build the economic security of the nation's young and thus the nation's future.

The Midrash relates the value God/Yahweh placed on children at Mount Sinai. Before God gave the people of Israel His Law, Yahweh required good guarantors. As guarantor, the Israelites first proposed their elders, but God deemed them insufficient. God also rejected their prophets as insufficient guarantors. Only when the people of Israel promised God that their children would be the keepers of His law did God agree to entrust them with His Law.[2]

It was a poor child that those of us who are Christians believe God used more than a millenium later as His messenger of good news to the poor. Yet at a time when, we are told, there is a religious revival and a return to more traditional and solid values, the world continues to kill millions of poor children each year, quite legally, through preventable malnutrition and infection.

Poverty is the greatest child killer in the affluent United States of the mid-1980s.[3] More American children die each year from poverty than from traffic fatalities and suicide combined. Over a five-year period, more American children die from poverty than the total number of American battle deaths during the Vietnam War. Yet our national leaders have invested $3.5 billion in research for a new "Star Wars" system to make our defenses impenetrable against enemy missiles in space, while thousands of American infants are dying in our cities and rural areas from preventable infant mortality.

The national death rate for infants between one month and one year of age—postneonatal mortality—actually increased by 3 percent between 1982 and 1983. Black babies saw their postneonatal mortality rate increase 5 percent, the first rise in eighteen years. In 1983 the ratio between white and black infant mortality rates was at its highest since 1940. A black infant in Chicago or Detroit or Cleveland is more likely to die in the first year of life than an infant in Cuba or Costa Rica.

Investing in Our Children and for Ourselves

Despite a national debt of $2 trillion (which children did not cause); despite Gramm-Rudman-Hollings; despite uncertainties in the national and international economies; despite misguided national leaders who believe that the American future rests in the stars rather than in the family, in missiles rather than mothers, in bombs rather than babies, in tanks rather than teachers—now is the time to adopt new preventive investment strategies to build healthy children, self-sufficient youth, and economically secure families.

As adults we are responsible for meeting the needs of children. It is our moral obligation. We brought about their births and their lives, and they cannot fend for themselves.

Children are utterly dependent on adult society to meet their most basic needs so they can survive and thrive and grow into self-sufficient adults—caring parents, competent workers with a fair opportunity for success and fulfillment, responsible citizens in a democracy. They need our help to be born healthy and at normal birth weight, which means that every mother must receive early and continuous prenatal health care and nutrition. They need adult society to meet their needs for food, shelter, and clothing. They need to grow up in an environment that is both secure and stimulating. And they need our help to get the education they require to prepare to compete in the world of work, to make sound decisions about when to become parents, to feel valued and valuable, and to feel that there is a fair chance to succeed.

We do not extend help to children solely because of moral obligations. It is also because we have faith in the future of our society, in its progress, its values, and its traditions, and we want our children to have every possible opportunity to participate in the society and contribute to it.

And we also fulfill our responsibilities to children because we know that the time will come when we will expect them to reciprocate. As we grow older, we will depend on them increasingly to meet our own needs. Because of dramatic social changes in the past century, our future comfort depends not just on our own children but on all American children. In general, we no longer expect our own children to support us directly when they are adults and we are elderly. Rather, we rely on Social Security and Medicare and Medicaid payments, which are funded by all Americans. Many of us will require the contributions of the next generation as a whole, and that generations's children. It is therefore in our self-interest to ensure that not just our own children but their contemporaries and their children are healthy, educated, productive, and compassionate. The United States needs every potential Abraham Lincoln, George Washington Carver, Ronald McNair, Mary McLeod Bethune, Barbara McClintock, and Henry

Cisneros it can develop in order to maintain its competitiveness in the twenty-first century and to support an increasingly aging population.

Our children are not only a precious resource but an increasingly scarce one. Until recently, America's youth population has been relatively plentiful, allowing our society to survive and our economy to grow, despite the waste of many young lives through society's neglect. We no longer have that margin for error. The ratio of workers to retirees has shrunk and will continue to shrink in the coming decades. One in three of those potential workers is minority.

In the next century we will need the contributions of every child in the United States today. Yet we are far from meeting our national and community responsibilities to all children to make that possible. This is a perilous course, for the future is being shaped right now. The potential high school graduate in the year 2000 is now a preschooler. One in four of today's preschool children is poor; one in nine is living in a household with income less than half of the poverty level. Only 16 percent of these eligible poor children are enrolled in Head Start, and only half can expect to be given compensatory education when they go to elementary school in the next couple of years. One child in six lives in a female-headed household, one in eight has no health insurance, and one in ten has not seen a doctor in the past year. One in two has a working mother, but only one in five has adequate day care. One in six lives in a family where no parent has a job, one in five is likely to become a teen parent, and one in seven is likely to drop out of school.

We invest in children because the cost to the public of sickness, ignorance, neglect, dependence, and unemployment over the long term exceeds the cost of preventive investment in health, education, employed youth, and stable families.[4]

· It costs $47 for a complete set of immunizations for a child. It costs an estimated $25,000 per year to keep a mentally retarded child in an institution. The nation saved an estimated $1 billion in the first decade of measles immunization efforts. It is poor fiscal policy to have less than half of black preschoolers fully immunized.

- It costs $600 to provide a mother with comprehensive prenatal care and thus to grow healthier babies; it costs more than $1,000 per day to keep low birth weight babies alive through neonatal intensive care.[5]

- It costs an average of $40 to provide a child the needed preventive checkups for an entire year under Medicaid; it averages $600 daily to hospitalize a child for an illness that could have been diagnosed and treated without hospitalization if there had been a routine preventive checkup.

- It costs $2,500 to give a child a year of Head Start or $3,000 to provide day care which enables a mother to work. It costs $4,200 to provide a year of AFDC benefits to a mother unable to find work or pay for day care.

- It costs $68 to provide family-planning services to a sexually active teen; it costs $3,000 to provide that teen and her baby prenatal care and delivery costs under Medicaid.

- It costs $600 to provide a year of compensatory education services to a teen; it costs more than $2,400 to finance a repeated grade for a disadvantaged student.

- It costs $495 per year to provide infant care through the Supplemental Food Program for Women, Infants, and Children (WIC); it costs an average of $12,000 to save a tiny newborn with neonatal intensive care.

- It costs $7,300 to provide a mother and two children with AFDC, housing assistance, food stamps, and energy-assistance benefits at 80 percent of the poverty level; it costs $8,000 to fund those two children in foster care when that mother becomes homeless or her apartment heatless.

- It costs $1,100 to provide a summer job for a teen; it costs $20,000 to keep that teen in a juvenile institution for a year.[6]

The premise of the American dream is that each succeeding generation will be better educated, housed, and employed than their parents. Yet in the 1980s we face economic stagnation, stalled progress in bringing poor and minority children and families into the mainstream of American society, and an underclass that threatens to become permanent for lack of targeted preventive and remediative policies.

These disturbing trends are reversible, through thoughtful public and private leadership that seeks a fairer balance between economic security for families to combat the internal enemies of hunger, homelessness, and joblessness and military security to combat external threats to national security; and between the desires and luxuries of the "haves" and the basic needs of the "have-nots" in American society. Such thoughtful leadership must begin with a recognition that the dichotomy conceptualized between a dependent underclass and a wholly self-sufficient middle and upper class is a myth.

Sharing the Responsibility—Family and Society

Parents in the United States bear the primary responsibility for meeting the needs of their own children. Rich or poor, most of them make every effort to give their children not only food, clothing, shelter, and health care, but the intangibles of self-esteem, motivation, and hope.

But American society is a complex organism, and no family shoulders this burden alone. Our nation invests in all children, from the day they are born. Not since the earliest frontier days have families not required and received some form of ongoing government assistance.[7] And even then, many got their start with land the government gave them. As American society has grown in complexity and interdependence, so, too, have government supports for families.

- Most American children are educated in public schools funded by the taxes of parents and nonparents alike. The formal education of children is a responsibility that we have decided should be shared.

- Taxpayers are allowed to deduct state and local tax payments for education from their income in figuring federal taxes if they itemize (as most high-income taxpayers do). In this way, the federal government makes its largest financial contribution to elementary and secondary education.

· Most American children who are able to pursue higher education receive large amounts of public support, either by enrolling in public institutions or by receiving government-subsidized grants or loans, or scholarships made possible by tax breaks. Our average public investment in the room, board, and tuition for *every* American student in higher education is over $8,000 a year.

· Millions of middle-income American families receive federal or state housing subsidies through programs such as Federal Housing Administration or Veterans Administration insurance and tax-exempt revenue bonds. Millions receive federal tax relief when they pay property taxes and make mortgage interest payments.

· Most American families pay many of their medical bills with the help of employer-provided health insurance, which the government subsidizes by not treating it as taxable income.

· Most American families live in neighborhoods that provide parks, libraries, playgrounds, and other enriching services underwritten by the government.

In these and myriad other ways, local, state, and federal governments invest in children and help support families. We do this to enhance, not to detract from, the role of the family. The relationship between family, community, and government is synergistic, strengthening both the family and the society in the complex undertaking of caring for children and building the future for them.

This partnership of family and government has roots far back in American history. To find its origins, we must reach back before the War on Poverty, before the New Deal, to the first federal funding for maternal and child health programs in 1921, to the Civil War era, and to the period before the adoption of the Constitution, when the Congress of the Confederation granted federal lands to help maintain public schools. I have included a list of just a few major programs to show how far back this partnership goes and how broad the support for it has been.

Our public schools, our public universities, our libraries and parks and playgrounds, our health insurance, our housing assistance, and our support for hospitals grow out of this tradition and are seemingly permanent parts of the social and political landscape. But our commitment to help the neediest children has seemed increasingly fragile and ephemeral in recent years. If we want to preserve their futures and our own, we will have to rededicate ourselves to government's side of the partnership, and we will have to do it soon. The government has never been a passive observer of the American economy, despite the current vogue for portraying it as such. Government at all levels must participate in redressing the child poverty crisis, just as it has participated in causing it. The multiple causes of this are all linked to our political and public life.

Children are poor because our nation has lost its moral bearings. We must work to change the national climate and focus attention on families and children. Recent federal government policy has spawned a new set of beatitudes which measure success not by how many needy pregnant women can be provided cost-effective prenatal care to prevent infant deaths and birth defects, but by how many families can be denied Medicaid and turned away from public health clinics. Not by how many hungry infants can be nourished, but by how many federal nutrition dollars can be held back as the waiting list of hungry babies grows. Not by how many poor homeless families are provided adequate shelter and minimum food, but by how many MX missiles we can find a hiding place for.

The current national rhetoric tells us it is more blessed to judge than to help the poor; that private charity is an adequate substitute for public justice; that it is proper for government to subsidize three-martini corporate lunches but improper for government to subsidize child care to help millions of poor working mothers escape welfare; that spending millions of dollars on golf outings and sports tickets and barber shops for defense contractors is a more justifiable national security expenditure than teaching poor chil-

Selected federal programs for children

1787	The Northwest Ordinance grants federal lands to the states to help maintain public schools.
1796	President Washington recommends the establishment of a national university.
1813	President Madison signs a law encouraging vaccination.
1857	President Buchanan signs a law incorporating the institution for the deaf and blind that later becomes Gallaudet College.
1862	President Lincoln signs the Morrill Act, granting land for colleges.
1865	President Lincoln signs a law creating the Freedmen's Bureau, providing 15 million food vouchers, clothing, income supplements, job training, energy assistance, and housing assistance for a quarter of a million families, and medical expense reimbursement for a million persons.
1874	President Grant signs the Padrone Act outlawing traffic in Italian children brought to the United States for exploitation as beggars.
1912	President Taft signs law creating the U.S. Children's Bureau "to investigate and report upon all matters pertaining to the welfare of children."
1917	President Wilson signs the Smith-Hughes Act to support vocational education.
1921	President Harding signs the Sheppard-Towner Act creating a federal-state program for maternal and infant health.
1933 & 1942	President Roosevelt signs laws providing federal funds for nursery schools and day care.
1935	President Roosevelt signs law creating Social Security, AFDC, and unemployment compensation.
1946	President Truman signs the National School Lunch Act.
1954	President Eisenhower signs amendments allowing the child care tax credit.
1958	President Eisenhower signs the National Defense Education Act to provide federal funds to public schools to improve training in science, mathematics, languages, and counseling, as well as funds for higher education student loans and other programs.
1961	President Kennedy signs a law creating the AFDC–Unemployed Parent program for two-parent families.

Selected federal programs for children

1964	President Johnson signs the Economic Opportunity Act, creating Head Start, Job Corps, and other educational and occupational training programs for children.
1965	President Johnson signs the Medicare and Medicaid law, as well as the Elementary and Secondary Education Act giving funds for school programs for children of low-income families.
1970	President Nixon signs the Education of the Handicapped Act.
1974	President Ford signs the Juvenile Justice and Delinquency Prevention Act and Runaway Youth Act.
1980	President Carter signs the Adoption Assistance and Child Welfare Act to assure major reforms in state foster care and child welfare services systems.

dren to read, write, and compute; that more government support for rich families strengthens them; while more government help for poor families weakens them, that a child's right to life ends at birth and does not include the right to adequate prenatal and nutritional care before birth or survival health, housing, and family supports after birth.

These perverse national values, hidden behind pro-family, "traditional values" rhetoric, are manifested in budget priorities that have cut billions each year since 1980 from survival programs for poor children and families. They are creating a new American apartheid between rich and poor, white and black, old and young, government and needy, corporation and individual, military and domestic needs—and have left millions of poor children to the wolves of hunger, homelessness, abuse, and even death.

Children are poor because their parents cannot find work. Today unemployment is at historically high levels, given the context of well over three years of economic recovery. In December 1985, thirty-seven months after the end of the 1981–82 recession, the official unemployment rate was still 6.9 percent. After the same amount of time had elapsed following the last big recession (1973–1975), the official unemployment rate was 6.1 percent.

Progressively higher unemployment rates have become the

norm. During each recession, unemployment climbs higher than during earlier recessions. During each period of recovery, unemployment drops, but not as far as it did during earlier recoveries. Unemployment now has topped 6.5 percent for well over seventy consecutive months, a phenomenon we have not seen since the Great Depression.

Millions of children remain locked in poverty because hardworking parents cannot make enough income to provide for their basic needs. Recent governmental and private sector policies have resulted not only in high unemployment but in low wages for those who are working, increasing poverty and making the struggle of poor families harder.

Among adults who are not disabled, elderly, or single parents nurturing small children, more than two-thirds of heads of poor households worked either full or part time during all or part of 1984. This includes more than half of all single heads of poor households and fully 80 percent of men who head poor households.

For a growing number of Americans, however, working does not mean escaping poverty. Lower-income children whose parents do work, even full time, are much more likely to wind up in poverty than at any other time in the recent past.

The erosion of the minimum wage by inflation is one major reason. In the past it was often raised to keep pace with inflation and provide a basic living standard for a small family. But since January 1981 it has been held at the same level, with the result that in real dollars (adjusted for inflation) a minimum-wage worker in 1986 took home less than four-fifths of what he or she earned in 1980. A full-time minimum-wage job now pays 75 percent of the poverty line for a family of three. Adjusting the minimum wage to inflation would help millions of children escape poverty.

The number of Americans working at inadequate wages has skyrocketed. In 1984 more than 11.4 million Americans with hourly wages were paid at such low rates (less than four dollars an hour) that income from a full-time job was too low to bring a family of three out of poverty. In 1979 the total with such inadequate wages was 2.8 million. Contributing factors to low wages for the working poor include increasing foreign competition, a shift

Full-time minimum-wage earnings as percentage of the poverty level for a family of three.

Year	Hourly minimum wage (dollars)	Annual dollar earnings for 2,000 hours work (50 weeks of 40 hours)	Poverty level (3 persons)	Full-time minimum wage earnings as percent of poverty level for 3 (%)
1964	1.25	2,500	$2,413	103.6
1969	1.60	3,200	2,924	109.4
1974	2.00	4,000	3,936	101.6
1979	2.90	5,800	5,784	100.3
1980	3.10	6,200	6,565	94.4
1981	3.35	6,700	7,250	92.4
1982	3.35	6,700	7,693	87.1
1983	3.35	6,700	7,938	84.4
1984	3.35	6,700	8,277	80.9
1985	3.35	6,700	8,589[a]	78.0
1986	3.35	6,700	8,934[a]	75.0

a. Estimated
Source: U.S. Bureau of the Census, "Money, Income, and Poverty Status of Families and Persons in the United States: 1984" (and same report for previous years).

from manufacturing to service jobs, and declining labor union effectiveness.

Poor families struggling to survive on meager wages have faced another burden: skyrocketing federal taxes. In 1979 a family of four with earnings at the poverty line paid less than 2 percent of its income in federal Social Security and income taxes. In 1986 that same family, if still earning (inflation-adjusted) poverty-line wages, has nearly 11 percent of its income taken by the federal government. Tax rates for single-parent families are even higher.

The huge tax cut passed in 1981 was structured to give all meaningful tax relief to the well-to-do. A family of four or more making poverty-line wages has been subjected to tax increases—not just in dollar amounts but in the portion of its earnings that the government takes—every year since 1979. Between 1980 and 1982 alone, the total federal tax drain on America's poor families grew by 58 percent. In 1985 a two-parent family with two children and poverty-level wages of $11,500 paid $1,221 in federal taxes—more than Boeing, ITT, General Dynamics, Transamerica, Grumman, Greyhound, or Lockheed paid in net federal corporate income taxes between 1981 and 1984.

As a result, more and more families have seen their impoverishment exacerbated rather than relieved by the federal government. This tax policy pushed hundreds of thousands of other families with very low incomes down into poverty. Poverty rates, which are figured on the basis of family income before taxes, leave out the millions more Americans—2.1 million members of families with children in 1984—who in reality are poor because, after taxes, their spendable incomes fall below the poverty line.

The new tax reform law reverses the damage done since 1979. After 1987 it will essentially restore the levels of federal taxation of the poor to 1979 levels. It does not give back any of the money unfairly taken from the poor in the last six years, nor solve the problem of egregiously high state and local taxes on the poor.

Children are poor because of decreasing government support at a time of increasing need, which has resulted from economic recession, unemployment, low wages, and increased taxes on the poor. The America of the 1980s presents a cruel paradox: while the rich are getting richer and often getting more government help, the poor are getting poorer and receiving less help. The decline in federal assistance for children has made living in poverty a harsher existence for 13 million children, and it has crippled the efforts of their families to struggle back up out of poverty.

The biggest cuts came in 1981, thanks to President Reagan's budget requests. That year Congress enacted cuts in programs for low-income families and children that totaled $10 billion a year for 1982 and a roughly equivalent amount for each subsequent year. Among the casualties were Medicaid, Maternal and Child Health programs, family-planning services, child immunizations, Aid to Families with Dependent Children, food stamps, school lunches and breakfasts, public housing for poor people, compensatory education to enable disadvantaged youngsters to keep up in school, and day-care services to enable poor and single and teen mothers to work. ⌐

In succeeding years President Reagan has asked for more huge cuts in children's programs. Since 1982, however, Congress has rejected those proposals, making small reductions in some programs in some years and modest increases or improvements in others. Congress seems to have awakened to the truth that repeatedly slashing survival programs for poor children is both unfair and short-sighted; accordingly, child and poor-family advocates have been able to avoid any large new cuts and restore over $3 billion of previously made cuts. But limiting the damage is not good enough. If Congress does not lead us forward, poor children will continue to slide backward. Even before the 1981 reductions, these programs were not adequate to meet the needs of America's poor children. Because of the growth of child poverty, many more children now need this help. And inflation continues to eat into funding levels, so that even flat funding for a program means that there is less and less available to the children who need it. In constant dollars (adjusted for inflation), a long list of programs serving children, youths, and families has been battered by cuts and freezes.

While the cuts in some of the larger income and health programs designed to help Americans weather unemployment and poverty have been smaller proportionally, their impact on the families' struggle to survive has been devastating. Moreover, many of these cuts were targeted on poor working families—those with incomes of $6,000 or $8,000 a year—making life as harsh for them as for other poor people and removing incentives to work. Other major cuts were aimed specifically at teenagers, withdrawing support during the crucial period when they are making the transition from high school to work, and making any effort to prevent teen pregnancy more difficult.

In an average month throughout most of the 1970s, about 40 to 50 percent of the jobless received unemployment benefits. In the 1980s, in part because of cuts in unemployment programs, the number of unemployed Americans receiving this help plummeted, reaching a record low in October 1985, when only 25.8 percent of the officially unemployed received benefits.

In difficult economic times more families would be expected to turn to AFDC as a last resort. But this program, too, was cut by making eligibility harder to obtain and benefits lower in real terms. In 1983 the average monthly AFDC payment per family was $312.88—65 percent of the level fifteen years earlier after adjusting for inflation. Only nineteen of the fifty states paid AFDC benefits (for a family of three) at 50 percent of the poverty line. And because of the combination of more restrictive program rules and an increase in the number of poor children, participation rates plummeted. In 1978 seventy-six children were on AFDC for every one hundred poor children in the country. In 1984 that ratio had dropped to fifty-five per one hundred.

Families requiring Medicaid to meet rising health-care costs have faced similar barriers. As services have been reduced and access to care constricted, the expenditures on behalf of each recipient child dropped sharply, from $470.91 in Fiscal Year (FY) 1979 to $406.08 in FY 1983 in constant (1983) dollars. In Medicaid, as in AFDC, many fewer children are now eligible when contrasted with the growing population of poor children. Seventy-five children were on Medicaid for every hundred poor children in the country in 1984. This is down from ninety-nine per hundred in 1976.

The only form of federal help to families that has increased consistently in recent years is assistance to families through tax breaks. Such help is important to middle- and upper-income families, but does extremely little for those poor families who need help the most.

- Tax subsidies for employer-paid health insurance do not help the children of an unemployed parent, or the children of a worker in a low-paying job that has no fringe benefits, or provides health coverage to the employee but not to his or her dependents. Such tax subsidies for the nonpoor have grown $3.5 billion per year, while federal spending for Maternal and

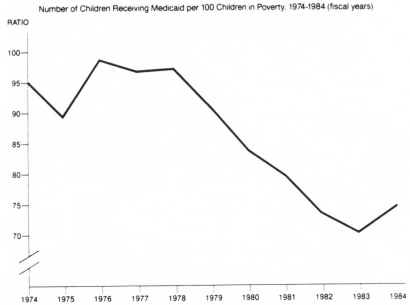

Number of Children Receiving Medicaid per 100 Children in Poverty, 1974-1984 (fiscal years)

Source: *A Children's Defense Budget: An Analysis of the FY 1987 Federal Budget and Children* (Washington, D.C.: Children's Defense Fund, 1986), p. 19.

Child Health programs was cut 18 percent and Medicaid served 700,000 fewer children.

Spending and tax subsidies for owner-occupied housing do not help a family too poor to own a home, or whose income is too low for the tax break to help. From 1979 to 1984 the cost in the tax system for the mortgage-interest break rose from about $8 billion to $23 billion. The federal budget for assistance through lower-income housing programs, however, followed precisely the opposite pattern, falling from $24 billion to $10 billion during those years.

The military joined the wealthy in fleecing programs for poor children. Since 1980, while poor children and families have lost $50 billion, the military budget has gained $624 billion. From 1987 to 1991, if the current administration has its way, children would lose another $33 billion in federal support. The Defense Department would gain another $385 billion in increases during this same period.

Real outlays per capita (1986 dollars) for national defense and for programs for low-income families and children.

Fiscal Year	National defense	Low-income programs[a]
1980	$ 785.03	$507.85
1981	828.70	516.99
1982	910.77	456.63
1983	991.72	466.14
1984	1,029.60	465.66
1985	1,092.68	470.12
1986	1,100.50	464.87
1987	1,112.07	431.07
1988	1,125.67	421.96
1989	1,163.81	411.15
1990	1,200.85	401.10
1991	1,238.69	400.15
Change:		
FY 1980–	+453.66	−107.70
FY 1991	+ 57.8%	− 21.2%

[a] Programs for low-income families and children include all outlays for education, training, and social service; health-care services (except Medicare); housing assistance; food and nutrition assistance; and other income security. Many small programs, such as library grants, are also included, as well as a few larger adult-education programs.

Sources: Figures for 1987–1991 are taken from the President's FY 1987 budget; figures for 1980–1986 are real outlays. The annual average level of the Consumer Price Index (CPI-W) for 1984–1991 is as shown in the FY 1987 budget. Total population estimates are from the U.S. Bureau of the Census.

Unless these misguided budget priorities are reversed, by 1990 every American will be spending 21 percent less on poor children and 58 percent more on the military than we did in 1980 (see table).

Children are poor because of demographic changes and the growth of female-headed families. In 1970 one baby in nine was born to a single mother. In 1983 one baby in five was. If the trends continue, by 1990 one out of five white babies and three out of four black babies will be born into female-headed households.

A new course is needed to invest more systematically in all poor families. Five steps must be taken immediately to meet some of the survival needs of poor children.

To combat infant mortality and low-birth-weight babies we should enact a new health initiative that would amend Medicaid. In 1986 Congress passed legislation which will allow states the option to extend coverage to (and get federal funding assistance for): poor pregnant women and children under age five whose family incomes are above AFDC payment levels but below the federal poverty level. It would cost no more than $200 million per year to extend this option to all children under age nineteen. One Stealth bomber costs $350 million. If we built one less than the 132 now planned, we could easily pay to extend Medicaid—with $150 million to spare.

In Head Start we should increase spending levels by $200 million a year for several years so we can reach at least 50 percent of eligible children, building quickly to the day when every eligible preschool child receives the benefit of an experience in Head Start or a comparable high-quality, comprehensive early-childhood development experience. Although the Stealth is supposed to replace the B-1 bomber, the House Armed Services Committee recently authorized a $200 million Strategic Bomber Contingency Fund, to buy components needed to continue to build the B-1, just in case. What we really need is $200 million invested in Head Start.

To relieve the tax burden on the poor, we sought to increase the value of the tax provisions most important to the poor and near-poor: the personal exemption, the standard deduction (also called the zero bracket amount), and, most important, the Earned Income Tax Credit. That credit is the only tax break of the hundreds in the tax code that is targeted solely for low-income families with children. The Tax Reform Act of 1986 is a good law for poor working families, and we are proud of CDF's part in it. But it does not help families with no earnings and it is only one step toward solving the child-poverty crisis. Many on both the right and the left feel they have completely discharged their obligations to American families by increasing the personal exemption from $1,000 (actually $1,080 in 1986) to $2,000.

Other pro-family tax issues, such as further necessary improvements in the Earned Income Tax Credit or more and better targeted tax relief for child-care costs, get short shrift from many of these "pro-family" advocates. Most noteworthy, the $1,000 increase in the personal exemption for every American, rich or poor, costs tens of billions of dollars, at a time when we are told there is no money to help the poor. We could have lifted *every* poor American out of poverty if we applied this money to targeted income-maintenance and jobs programs.

We need to upgrade the minimum wage immediately to $4.25 per hour, and then have it keep pace with inflation. This would actually lower federal government costs for welfare and related programs, while lifting hundreds of thousands of children out of poverty through their parents' wages. We must restore the concept of a family-supporting floor to wages.

There are many other things we can and must do. The common principle is that the problems of child/family poverty are not insoluble. In many ways they are not particularly difficult or particularly expensive to solve. We know some solutions from the experiences of the United States. We know others from the experiences of other countries; virtually every wealthy Western country suffers much less from child poverty and its consequences than we do. We know the way, but we need the will and the leadership.

Tragically, many of our leaders lack that will. They urge us to abandon our efforts to help our neediest children because, although we aimed a few government programs at the problems in the past decades, poverty did not disappear. These leaders ignore the drastic limitations on former efforts to help poor children. Our nation has not yet made a long-term, concentrated effort to eliminate poverty through jobs or an income policy (except for the elderly, whose poverty we have reduced dramatically through Social Security and Supplemental Security Income). Rather, we have created a network of marginal programs, each of which serves very limited groups of the poor, almost always with inadequate funding—food for some, medical care for others, compensatory education in some school years but not others, housing assistance for some, child care for a few, and so on.

The successes on which we can build are solid and inspiring. Despite their limitations, many of the specific public programs for children and youths—programs started by Presidents Madison, Lincoln, Taft, Wilson, Harding, Eisenhower, Nixon, and Carter, as well as by F. D. Roosevelt and Johnson—have worked well. Through them we transformed the lives of millions of children, from despair to hope, from sickness to health, from ignorance to learning. Instead of being defensive, we should be proud. But we have to do a much better job of letting the American people know that much of their investment in children and families and in specific social programs has not been wasted, contrary to current propaganda by those who seek to undermine all federal social programs, and that many of them make a significant positive difference.

By 1977 black and white high school graduates were entering college at equal rates. In the fifteen years after Medicaid began, black infant mortality dropped 49 percent, more than nine times the rate of improvement during the prior fifteen-year period. In 1963, before the creation and expansion of several federal public health programs, only 63 percent of pregnant women in America began prenatal care in the first trimester of pregnancy; by 1979 that figure had risen to 76 percent. The gains children who have been enrolled in Head Start have made—in elementary school, in high school, in higher education, and in the employment market—are well documented.

Poverty among children, both black and white, was reduced greatly during the 1960s.

· One out of ten of all American children was removed from poverty between 1960 and 1969. Black children and white children, children from one-parent homes and children from two-parent homes were being lifted above the poverty line at about the same rates. Although the improvement was strong from 1960 to 1965, when there was an economic boom, it was much stronger during 1966 to 1969, when there was both a boom and a War on Poverty.

After 1969 two major changes greatly hurt low-income families with children. The handful of provisions of the War on Poverty that were intended to reduce poverty immediately—the pressure on states to make inflation adjustments of AFDC benefit levels and the community-based employment provisions of Model Cities, for example—were repealed or abrogated. The economy underwent a series of price shocks and recessions that essentially eliminated all real dollar growth in hourly wages, while inducing high rates of inflation.

During the 1969 to 1979 period, states voluntarily increased AFDC levels by less than half the rate of inflation—and the federal government did not mandate any change at all. By the end of the decade, AFDC levels were so low that fewer children in poverty were eligible for AFDC than at the beginning. During that same decade President Nixon's Comprehensive Employment and Training Act (CETA) was offered as a substitute for Model Cities. But, until it was reformed in 1978, CETA simply avoided the poor, particularly the young black poor. (The program, abolished in 1981, essentially operated only in 1979 and 1980 as a targeted jobs program.)

Thus, children were slightly worse off in 1979 than in 1969. But from 1979 to 1983 the bottom fell out. In 1980, 1981, and 1982 more than 1 million children per year were added to the poverty rolls, and the rate of child poverty rose to its level from before the War on Poverty.

Two back-to-back recessions—the one in President Reagan's first term being the most severe since the Depression—and inadequate wages hit very hard at those families with low-income working parents. Since so high a proportion of the black families and female-headed families with children were already poor before the recessions hit, the relative impact was greatest among intact white families, who were typically above poverty until one parent lost his or her job. At the same time, federal budget cuts dropped about 700,000 children from AFDC and eliminated the CETA jobs that employed several hundred thousands of parents. Taken together, and that was just how America's children had to take them, the recessions and budget cuts were devastating to black and white children alike.

But during the 1970s two other trends continued as they had during the 1960s:

· The proportion of children in one-parent families grew for both white and black children. That growth actually started in the tranquil, nuclear-family 1950s. But during the 1960s economic progress was fast enough to more than offset the loss to children from family breakups. During the 1970s economic progress was very slight and could not offset the continuing losses of income brought about by the increasing proportion of children who were attached to only one adult.

· Also during the 1970s parents worked more. Mothers in two-parent families went to work, or worked longer hours. The parent in one-parent families also worked longer hours. Although parents did not increase their real dollars earned per hour, the additional hours worked did something to improve low family incomes. Thus, if we look only at children with one-parent families, the proportion in poverty fell slightly during the 1970s. However, the shift from two- to one-parent families more than offset these gains, and children as a whole became poorer. That was true both for white and for black children.

In every child who is born, under no matter what circumstances and of no matter what parents, the potentiality of the human race is born again and in him, too, once more and of each of us, our terrific responsibility toward human life: toward the utmost idea of goodness, of the horror of terror, and of God.

—James Agee,
Let Us Now Praise Famous Men

3 · Preventing Adolescent Pregnancy

Adults disagree about the nature of the teenage pregnancy problem. Some see it as primarily a moral problem; others as an economic or poverty problem. Some are concerned because of its implications for family development, infant mortality, and health outcomes; others because it contributes to school dropout and dependency.

There is just as much disagreement about solutions. Some see the problem only as an issue of sex education and family planning; others as a problem requiring comprehensive and long-term education and economic solutions. Some think it just a parental responsibility; others believe that a broad partnership between families, community institutions, and government will be necessary to set all our young people on the right path.

A majority of Americans agree, however, that teen pregnancy is a serious problem. Indeed, it is epidemic among all races and classes of American youth today. It could happen to your daughter, your niece, your grandchild, your friend's child, unless all Americans begin to think of ways to help children avoid premature sexual activity, pregnancy, and parenthood.

Each day more than 3,000 girls get pregnant and 1,300 give birth. Twenty-six thirteen- and fourteen-year-olds have their first child, thirteen sixteen-year-olds have their second child. Each year, 1.1 million American teen girls—one in ten—become pregnant.[1] That is more than the entire Massachusetts school enrollment. Over half a million teenage girls have babies, a number nearly equal to the total population of the city of Boston. More disturbing is the pregnancy increase among younger teens. Each year, 125,000 girls fifteen and under become pregnant.

According to data from the Alan Guttmacher Institute, the United States leads nearly all developed nations of the world in rates of teenage pregnancy, abortion, and child-bearing, even though it has roughly comparable rates of teen sexual activity.[2] The data show that our top-ranked status does not result only from the high rates of pregnancy and parenthood among minority teens. The pregnancy rates for white teenagers are twice as high as those of Canada, France, and England. Moreover, the maximum difference in birth rates occurs among girls under the age of fifteen, the most vulnerable teenagers.

The costs of adolescent parenthood are enormous—for the teen parents, for their children, and for society.

· Forty percent of teenage girls who drop out of school do so because of pregnancy or marriage. Only half of the teens who become parents before the age of eighteen graduate from high school.

· A teen parent earns half the lifetime earnings of a woman who waits until age twenty to have her first child.

· Teen mothers are twice as likely to be poor as are nonteen mothers. Babies born to single mothers are two and a half times more likely to be poor than those born to two-parent families.

· Only 54 percent of all teen mothers in 1983 began prenatal care in the first three months of pregnancy. Babies of mothers who receive late or no prenatal care are three times more likely to die in their first year of life than those who receive early care.

· Babies born to teens represented about 14 percent of all births in 1983, but 20 percent of all low-birth-weight births. Low-birth-weight babies are twenty times more likely to die in the first year of life and special hospital care for low-birth-weight babies averages $1,000 a day.

· Medicaid pays for 30 percent of all hospital deliveries involving pregnant teens, at an annual cost of about $200 million a year.

· In 1985 half a million babies were born to teenage girls. The public cost was $1.4 billion dollars.

The international data make it clear that these costs are not the inevitable outcomes of increased adolescent sexual activity, but of our inability as a society to deal in a preventive way with the implications of that increase: to provide early comprehensive sex and family-life education in our homes, schools, and other institutions and to give sexually active teens access to family-planning services and counseling. The United States laments its high numbers of teen pregnancies but winds up providing for large numbers of teen parents and their children because we do not encourage early parental and other appropriate adult communication with children about the consequences of too early sexual activity, and we refuse to give our teens the capacity to delay parenthood, while unsuccessfully imploring too many of them, too late, to delay sexual activity. These data demonstrate the bankruptcy of such a policy—or lack of it. Withholding sex education and family-planning services has *not* led to less teenage sexual activity in the United States. Conversely, the provision of this information and service in Europe and Canada has resulted not in increased sexual activity but in heightened sexual responsibility.

Adopting the approach to pregnancy prevention taken by our European counterparts will help reduce the rates of teen pregnancy and parenthood. We need to encourage a national atmosphere, in a wide range of settings, of open parental and responsible adult communication with the young about sexuality. State mandates for family-life education and the development of decision making skills in the schools should begin in early childhood and continue through the high school years. At present only a minority of students receive timely and comprehensive sex or family-life education in the schools. The norm in the United States is definitely too little too late. Fewer than one school district in five offers students in-depth discussion of such basic issues as the responsibilities of parenthood, the consequences of teen pregnancy, or how to resist peer pressure for sex, before the ninth grade. And four out of every ten sexually active teens who need contraceptive counseling and services are not receiving help from a clinic or private doctor.

But "capacity-building strategies" alone—appropriate sex education for all children and youth and contraception for sexually active teens—are not enough. The costs of adolescent parenthood fall disproportionately on those least able to support them: teens from low-income or minority families; teens with poor basic skills and poor employment potential. Of course ascribing each of these "costs" to teen pregnancy may oversimplify the matter, as politicians and social policy analysts are wont to do, especially at a time of cutbacks and putative cost-consciousness. There are limits to what each of these facts tell us. For example, a teen parent has only a fifty-fifty chance of graduating from high school, and will earn only half of what a woman who waits until age twenty to have her first child will earn. But teen parenthood disproportionately occurs to those who are also, independently, more likely to drop out and less likely to earn high wages. *Any* poor teenager is three or four times more likely to drop out of school than a nonpoor teen. And *any* woman without a high school diploma will earn only 41 percent of the lifetime earnings of a woman with a college degree. Teen parenthood clearly exacerbates these problems, raises these costs. But it is also quite clearly one cause, one cost, one effect, one manifestation, of many growing out of childhood poverty. These are interacting causes and effects.

As an analogy to the higher teen pregnancy rates among poor adolescent girls, including, because they are disproportionately poor, minority girls, consider the higher crime rates among poor adolescent boys, including, because they are disproportionately poor, minority adolescents. We recognize the cost of crime to its victims, or the cost of incarceration, and other costs. Most of us also recognize that the syndrome is one of poverty, broken families, bad schools, high dropout rates, low job and economic expectations, and criminal activity intermingling as part of a single complex pattern of cause and effect. While we want to prevent adolescent pregnancy, as we want to prevent delinquency, and want and expect teenagers and their families to take responsibility for their lives, we also must recognize the powerful social causes at work and deal with them so that the teens have real options and expectations that give them a realistic chance to exercise that responsibility.

A recent analysis of data from the National Longitudinal Survey of Young Americans, prepared for CDF by Dr. Andrew Sum of Northeastern University, found that American teenagers who are poor and who lack basic academic skills are almost six times more likely to become pregnant than their more affluent and more skilled peers, regardless of race.[3] Many of these teens lack the capacity to delay parenthood, although they initiate sexual activity a little earlier than more advantaged teens. Their poorer access to information and services exacerbates the effects of any sexual activity. But many of these teens also lack the motivation to delay parenthood. That is why hope and opportunity and a sense of usefulness are the primary contraceptives this nation must provide for all its young.

A major change in the nature of a child's decisionmaking process occurs once a teen becomes sexually active. From that point on the teen must make repeated affirmative decisions to prevent pregnancy; unless decisions are made, unwed parenthood is the natural outcome. Teens, like adults, must decide to use contraception; once pregnant, decide to abort or place the child up for adoption or keep the baby; and, if keeping the baby, decide to marry to legitimize the birth. (Most teen marriages are formed for this reason, although teen marriages are twice as likely to end in separation or divorce than are post-teen marriages.) These are not easy decisions to make alone. The failure of an adult society to help teens weigh the pros and cons of each decision leads to inexcusably high rates of unintended pregnancies, abortions, births, and single-parent families. Furthermore, if we leave this complex decisionmaking, fact-finding, and service finding to teens, we guarantee that at each point the gap will widen between those with incentives to delay parenthood (such as being able to go on to college or to graduate with one's class) and the less fortunate teens for whom the future holds few opportunities that would be diminished by early parenthood.

Why Adolescent Pregnancy Is a Problem

Teen pregnancy and parenthood is as old as teen sex. What has changed dramatically is the utility or nonutility to the culture of teen sex and child-bearing. As a result of socioeconomic change, we no longer want teens to give birth and have imposed a moralistic overlay. Adolescent parenthood is no longer a viable option for thriving and progressing in society. As recently as the turn of the century, as in earlier times, youth generally finished school around the time of the onset of physical maturity, entered the work force as adults while in their teens, and had families by their late teens. By the 1940s, however, the schooling process for the middle class was stretching into the early twenties. Today half of our young adults are still in school at the age of nineteen. Only half have entered the labor force as nonstudents at age twenty. Half are still unmarried at age twenty-four, and half of the women twenty-five years and under have not borne their first child. The educational and social maturation process, as a foundation for economic self-sufficiency, extends well into the twenties. But for too many youth, economic reality, particularly if accompanied by unintended pregnancy, grinds this process to a halt and makes economic success a distant dream.

A single parent under twenty-five is nine times as likely to be poor as a young woman living on her own without children. Three-quarters of all single mothers under that age live in poverty. With more than half of all teen mothers raising their children alone, and with those who are married facing higher rates of separation and divorce, the costs of teenage parenthood—to the parents, to the children, and to society in terms of money spent and productivity lost—are too great to ignore.

Teenage pregnancy is a problem because it very often precludes the completion of education, the securing of employment, and the creation of a stable relationship, and because it makes the completion of each of these transitional steps more difficult. It is a problem because we no longer live in an America in which eighteen- and nineteen-year-old men can earn enough to support a family, and because we have never had an America in which the average single woman with children could earn a decent wage at any age. Meanwhile, young men, especially young black men, are increasingly unable to fulfill a traditional role as breadwinner and are less willing to accept their responsibilities as fathers. In 1970 three teen births out of ten were to single mothers. In 1983 this number had increased to more than five out of ten.

In 1984, 65 percent of teen hourly workers and 29 percent of hourly workers in their early twenties could not make wages sufficient to raise an intact, one-income family with a child out of poverty. And that is the proportion of those who were employed. Among black males, only 59 percent were employed in January of 1986; among black teen males only 21 percent were employed.

Contrary to popular perception, the majority of teen parents (342,283 of 499,038 in 1983) are white. Poor and minority teens, however, have a disproportionate share of teen births and are disproportionately affected by the social and economic consequences of early parenthood. A black teen is twice as likely to become pregnant as a white teen. A black teen is five times as likely as a white teen to become an unwed parent. This is primarily, albeit not completely, correlated to higher poverty rates among black teens. Nor is teen pregnancy just an urban, big-city problem. The ten worst states for percentage of teen out-of-wedlock births are overwhelmingly Southern states that are typically less urbanized.[4]

Adolescent pregnancy is everybody's problem in every part of the United States. The black community knows it has a disproportionate problem and is taking steps to respond. The white community has to understand that it, too, has a problem, as white families are now beginning to reflect the patterns of black families twenty years ago. The white teen birth rate has increased slightly, while the black teen birth rate has decreased.

Ways to Prevent Teen Pregnancy

Preventing teen pregnancy requires investing in comprehensive efforts to bolster the motivation as well as the capacity of teens to prevent premature sexual activity and pregnancy. We must give them hope, opportunity, information, and skills. Five areas are extremely important in accomplishing this.

Many and varied opportunities for success. Children and teens need to feel good about themselves. They need a clear vision of a successful and self-sufficient future. Self-sufficiency potential is related to self-esteem. Self-esteem can be built both through academic and nonacademic experiences. For youth who are not doing well in school, nonacademic avenues for success may be crucial.

Building academic skills. Teenagers who are a grade behind or have poor basic skills or poor attendance are at high risk of early parenthood. Low-income and minority teens have higher rates of school failure. A sound education for all, beginning in early childhood, must be a strong priority.

Work-related skill-building and work exposure. Employment success is related to work attitudes, occupational knowledge, and work-place exposure, as well as basic competencies and specific job-related skills. Teens who perform poorly in school and become teenaged parents often have poor work-related skills and, because of lack of exposure to work-place norms, have behavioral patterns maladapted to the employment market.

Family-life education and life planning. All teens need education about sexuality and parenthood and help in integrating that information into their thinking about themselves and their futures. We need age-appropriate family-life education for students from kindergarten through twelfth grade in all states, and we need to encourage parents and religious institutions to communicate more effectively with the young about sexuality.

Comprehensive adolescent health services. All sexually active teens—and, increasingly, preteens—need access to contraception. Our failure to provide such services is only one element of our broader neglect of the health needs of adolescents. The relatively poor health status of high-risk teens and preteens and their poor linkage with the health-care system demonstrate that family-planning services and counseling are among the many services that must be provided in the broader context of primary adolescent health care.[5]

A range of comprehensive and convenient services for teenagers, in and out of school settings, must be provided to build on the successful experiences of comprehensive school-based clinics that have both improved the access of teens to general health care and have decreased rates of both first and second pregnancies among participating teens. School-based clinics constitute only a fraction of adolescent clinics. The majority of the services they provide are not related to family planning. Of the sixty-one school-based clinics, less than one-third dispense contraceptives on site. The oldest, in St. Paul, Minnesota, has succeeded in reducing first teen pregnancies from eighty per thousand to twenty-nine per thousand, and repeat pregnancies to 1.4 percent, compared to 33 percent nationally. The St. Paul clinic also has been responsible for an increase to 87 percent of pregnant students graduating, compared to 50 percent nationally.

Such steps cannot be taken overnight. They must be adapted to the needs of different communities and target populations. They require commitment, resources, and patience. Adolescent pregnancy is not a single problem affecting a single group of teens for the same reasons, in the same ways, or with the same consequences. We must break down this complicated problem by race, age, class, and gender and then design appropriate outreach and remedies for each group, meanwhile realizing how these varied strategies add up to a comprehensive whole.

More importantly, we must create a national and community climate that makes teen pregnancy prevention a leading national priority and involves all elements of American society in its solutions.

A survey conducted for CDF in July 1985 shows that there is a greater awareness of the problem of teenage pregnancy and greater enlightenment about causes and solutions than is generally assumed. Some 1,813 adult respondents, aged eighteen and over, were interviewed. They were 85 percent white, 10 percent black, 53 percent Protestant, and 28 percent Catholic; 50 percent of them had incomes of $20,000 or more. Two-thirds of the poll respondents classified teen pregnancy as a serious problem. Poor parenting, not enough education and information about sex and birth control, and changes in morals were the top three reasons given by them to the question of why adolescent pregnancy is a problem in the United States. Guidance, supervision, and education, particularly in the face of changes in sexual mores over the past few decades, were seen as the areas most ripe for change. Two-thirds agreed that increased information regarding sex and birth control is a more realistic solution than seeking (or hoping for) abstinence. And a majority recognized that giving teenagers other ways to feel good about themselves is the best solution.

The survey results indicate a climate of public opinion that is positively disposed to a serious discussion of teen pregnancy, as well as a willingness to take steps to solve the problem. It is not yet one of the most prominent issues on the American public agenda, but the vast majority of the public are aware of the problem on an individual and social level. Efforts to heighten awareness coupled with sensitive and sensible approaches to begin tackling the problem should meet with considerable public support.

The solutions suggested by policy analysts, including such seemingly controversial ones as sex education and contraception, did not trouble the respondents. The exception was abortion, clearly the most controversial issue, which received virtually no support as a solution to teen pregnancy. Although most solutions to teen pregnancy are not particularly disturbing to the American public, they will be cast as such by a well-orchestrated opposition. Anticipating and neutralizing that opposition and educating the media, adults, and other opinion-setting groups must be a top priority.

The CDF Program for Adolescent Pregnancy Prevention

Each year CDF proposes a new initiative in a sequential program that over time will add up to a comprehensive and cumulative approach to teen pregnancy prevention. In 1983 we began consciousness-raising and networking about the dimensions and implications of the teen pregnancy problem. We began with black women leaders and then expanded to additional networks of black and white and Hispanic leaders. This process will be a continuing one until we reach enough of a critical mass of policymakers and community and organizational leaders to make the prevention of teenage pregnancy a national priority.

A problem cannot be solved until it is identified and understood. In 1984 CDF launched Adolescent Pregnancy Child Watch in collaboration with the Association of Junior Leagues, the National Council of Negro Women, the March of Dimes, and the National Coalition of 100 Black Women. Child Watch trains local volunteers and helps them conduct needs assessments of the teen pregnancy problem in their communities and consider appropriate ways to respond locally. Phase I of Child Watch is in various stages of being completed in sixty-four communities in thirty-one states. Phase II action projects are beginning in about fifteen communities. Forty new project leaders will be trained during 1987 from a much larger number of new communities that are seeking to become involved.

Child Watch is a recognition that preventing teen pregnancy requires the involvement of broad-based community coalitions to find local solutions to inform and complement state and national responses. Child Watch projects understand the importance of collaborative, comprehensive, and long-term actions in combatting teen pregnancy.[6]

In 1985 CDF launched a five-year prenatal care campaign, which has seen significant results in a few targeted communities, including a new $91 million health care package for the indigent in the state of Texas. Each year CDF publishes a *Maternal and Child Health Data Book*, documenting by state and race the status of such health indicators as infant mortality, teen and out-of-wedlock births, and prenatal care.

The purposes of the prenatal care campaign are fivefold: (1) to expand funding for and access to prenatal care for adolescent and poor mothers; (2) to educate communities—teens, parents, community groups, and providers—about the importance of ensuring that young mothers receive care; (3) to involve a range of community and public decisionmakers in setting and implementing goals to make certain that the far-too-high number of babies born to mothers who receive no prenatal care decreases significantly over the next five years; (4) to draw teen mothers into the health-care system and prevent repeat pregnancies; and (5) to get people concerned with teen pregnancy to work together and build a broad agreement on a response that is sensible, noncontroversial, and cost-effective as well as critically important to infant mortality and teen pregnancy prevention.

In 1986 CDF launched a five-year multimedia campaign, whose first phase is aimed at adults, to raise public consciousness on the teen pregnancy issue. Subsequent targeted campaigns, utilizing radio as well as TV and print, will be directed toward various groups of teens. Poster, transit ads and billboards, and 60-, 30-, and 15-second TV public service announcements constitute the first phase. NBC, CBS, and Fox television stations air the spots. The transit campaign was started in eight cities: Atlanta, Chicago, Detroit, Jacksonville, Kansas City, Minneapolis, Philadelphia, and Washington. Other communities have been adopting it, and, as of July 1986, participating localities also included Madison, Wisconsin, Norfolk, Virginia, Portland, Oregon, and Cuyahoga County, Ohio.

In response to the growing public awareness and interest in a range of strategies to prevent teen pregnancy, CDF has established an Adolescent Pregnancy Prevention Clearinghouse, which provides ongoing information and technical assistance. Six bi-monthly Clearinghouse publications about effective models and activities on various aspects of the teen pregnancy problem are published each year.[7]

In addition, a first-step policy menu for federal and state legislators and executives has been developed. This agenda is designed to build self-sufficient youth with a stake in the future. The importance of going beyond sex education and family planning to improving life options by ensuring a decent education, job training, and jobs for all our youth is stressed. If we do not take a self-sufficiency, skills-building approach, we are simply creating slightly older female-headed families, which still lack the economic and educational means to support themselves. Babies with twenty-three-year-old uneducated, single poor mothers, rather than sixteen-year-old uneducated, single poor mothers is not the outcome we seek.

Examples of the kind of policies state and federal governments could consider and adopt are included in a Children's Survival Bill, which has been introduced in the Congress and which has been shared with every member of Congress and every governor through our annual publication: *A Children's Defense Budget: An Analysis of the FY 1987 Federal Budget and Children.*[8]

To supplement these ongoing national and local public education, networking, technical assistance, and policy development activities, CDF is developing an intensive, long-term, and comprehensive hands-on demonstration effort in a very few local target sites to show that teen pregnancy rates can be lowered. The local site effort will enable CDF to gain experience in identifying and implementing local solutions to adolescent pregnancy problems that can inform our national and state policy efforts. Too often national and state policy development is not tested for real-life implementation barriers. Too often successful local models lack mechanisms and funding for continuation or broader adaptation. We envision a minimum five-year effort in selected cities, which will be chosen by the end of 1987.

Making a significant dent in any major social problem requires a lot of hard work and persistence over a long period of time; endless trial and error; constant testing, refining, and mixing of strategies; flexible responses to changing times, new needs and targets of opportunity; and systematic, step-by-step movement toward long-term goals.

These goals must be:

- to reduce the incidence of first teen pregnancies;
- to reduce the incidence of repeat teen pregnancies;
- to reduce the number of teen school dropouts as a result of pregnancy and parenting;
- to reduce the number of babies born to poor mothers who have not received comprehensive prenatal care.

How to target our efforts, set and track specific percentage goals, is a complicated process. Do we focus on the nine states that produce half of all teen births? Do we pick sites where the problem may be less severe but where chances of initially designing innovative successful remedies are more likely? Do we focus on reducing pregnancy and birth rates among girls sixteen and younger? Do we put substantial effort into neglected males or leave that to other groups, such as the Urban League? Do we focus primarily on poor and minority children, or must we develop a more balanced set of overlapping strategies for poor and middle-class youth in order to broaden the political base for change? What kind of non-stifling evaluation procedures do we build into local projects and national policy development? Who should do it?

Establishing outcome criteria, as opposed to organizational and community awareness and involvement goals which characterized our first five years' effort, is the task before us. With the help of an advisory board of adolescent pregnancy specialists we are grappling with that job.

Pitfalls to Avoid

Moralizing. Some of us point judgmental fingers at others or assume that one age group, class, or race has a corner on morality. Such attitudes obscure causes and effects and can lead to backlash rather than cooperation and change. Moralizing will not solve the teen pregnancy problem. But moral adult examples and efforts to provide constructive alternatives to young people can help.

Using teen pregnancy as another excuse to batter the poor. Research by Mary Jo Bane and William Wilson indicates that welfare is not the cause of teenage pregnancy.[9] Teen pregnancy rates are higher in states with the lowest welfare benefits and lowest in states with higher welfare benefits. Most teen pregnancies are unwanted or unplanned.

Quick fixes. The media and too many politicians and citizens are looking for magic bullets or quick results to complex problems. Preventing teen pregnancy and alleviating the poverty of female-headed households are a long-haul battle, which we must fight systematically and step by step.

Despair. Our biggest initial task is to pierce the veil of despair, provide a glimmer of hope for young people going nowhere in our society, identify efforts that seem to be making a difference, and package them in ways that a majority of the American public can support.

Stereotyping. At all costs we must resist a national inclination to define the complex problem of teen pregnancy as one peculiar to a black "underclass," and to act as if welfare is the main cause or consequence of this social phenomenon which affects many different target groups in different ways and which will respond to a range of outreach strategies and remedies. The families portrayed in the media too often are one slice of the black family crisis that must be addressed by the black community and by the nation. But there are other slices of black and white youth and family reality about whom we do not hear: the many millions of children in poor families who are not on welfare or who are coping despite teen pregnancy and other barriers of poverty; the many poor children who do not get pregnant at all; and the millions of middle-class teens, black and white, male and female, who need the same parental communication and value transfusion that poor children also need.

Political carelessness. Our goal must be to win for children and poor teenagers. In order to do this, we must emphasize the issues that unite rather than divide us. If there is more than one way to achieve a result, and one road has a lot of political traffic while another has less or none, take the latter road. Social reformers need to anticipate better the political opposition and figure out ways of going around it, wherever possible. But we should also be prepared to fight and to do the careful political organizing that ensures victory despite controversy. Too often we let a few noisy people scare us away from fighting for programs that children need. We can organize and fight as effectively as they can if all of us are willing to make the effort.

A lack of confidence and patience. We must not fear testing a variety of approaches until we hit upon the combination that works. Social-reform strategies are not different from the scientific method; it is trial and error, trial and error. We must avoid unrealistic expectations for ourselves and others. Comprehensive, long-term efforts are essential to recapture the future for today's youth. Few, if any, major social reforms, whether child labor protection or dismantling legally entrenched racial segregation, whether female suffrage or black voting rights, have accrued in the absence of a long and arduous struggle, usually lasting decades.

The pace of American life has quickened, and perhaps social problems develop more quickly than they used to. Certainly public attention is more ephemeral than it used to be. But strengthening families and preventing teen pregnancy requires the same concerted effort over the long term as did earlier struggles for social progress. A setback this month, this year, means little. The struggle will take many years. Nothing less will make a real difference.

New laws are not enough. The emergency we now face is economic, and it is a desperate and worsening situation. For the 35 million poor people in America, there is a kind of strangulation in the air. In our society it is murder, psychologically, to deprive a man of a job or an income. You are in substance saying to that man that he has no right to exist.

—Martin Luther King, Jr.

4 · Supporting Families: Jobs and Income

The belief that we need to reform the American welfare system is once again in vogue. Genuine welfare reform is long overdue. Fundamental improvements in our current system of cash and in-kind transfer payments can and must be made.

I strongly suspect, however, that what I mean by welfare reform is different from what President Reagan means or what Ed Meese, who is in charge of the Administration's efforts in this regard, will recommend. Today's call for welfare reform is coming against a background—to which the administration has contributed mightily—of blaming welfare for the situation of the poor and for the crisis of the American family, in particular the black family.

If we are going to accomplish true welfare reform, we must know what welfare should—and should not—be blamed for. And if we are going to accomplish true welfare reform, we must understand the broader contexts of how the job market works, of how poor and working-class families get by, and of how welfare is one small part of government aid to families—though the part we single out for criticism and stigma.

We must not allow our focus on the complex task of reforming the welfare system to obscure our vision of attaining broader family economic security. What we call welfare is only a small part of the array of public policy that promotes—or undercuts—family economic security, self-sufficiency, and cohesion. Reexamining the welfare system must be only one part of the effort to reassess how we meet the needs of America's families and children. To focus on welfare reform as the only response to the family crisis or to child and family poverty in this nation is dangerously short-sighted and doomed to failure.

Welfare Myths

Let us start by looking at the main focus of all this consternation: Aid to Families with Dependent Children. The AFDC program takes less than 1 percent of all federal government expenditures. It is the critical source of support for one out of fifteen Americans, yet we devote to it one-two hundred and fifty-fifth of our Gross National Product (GNP).

The 8.6 billion federal dollars we spent on AFDC in 1985 was certainly not a trivial amount, but it was small relative to other parts of the government and the economy. For every dollar the federal government spent on AFDC, it spent twenty-two on Social Security, eight on Medicare, three on farm programs, and eleven on veterans benefits and military personnel and retirement programs. The $8.6 billion is only a little larger than the 1984 profits of IBM ($6.9 billion) or General Motors ($5.5 billion).

AFDC may represent a tiny fraction of our GNP, but it consumes a far larger share of our public debate and contributes to an even larger share of the right wing's anxieties. It and related programs are being portrayed as a vast and powerful engine of social destruction: we are told that welfare causes promiscuity and illegitimacy, laziness and dependency, creates an underclass, discourages work, and generally causes a vastly disproportionate share of the ills of the poor, and of society as a whole.

The facts do not support these views. Our welfare system is far from ideal, but it is even further from being a vast engine of social destruction. It is, however, a vast engine of social mythology. I think it has become such an engine because it is tied up with American problems with class, race, gender roles, and sexuality. This becomes clearer when one looks at the myths that permeate the welfare debate.

The first myth is that welfare is a huge drain on the public purse. I have just cited figures showing that this is not true, at least in terms of AFDC expenses. The corollary myth—that the poor on welfare live too well—is also belied by the figures. In 1986 combined AFDC and food-stamp benefits were below the poverty level in every state and less than 75 percent of the poverty level in forty states. In Mississippi a nonworking family of three got $120 per month in AFDC and $204 in food stamps. In Tennessee, $153 and $195; in Arkansas, $192 and $183.

The present administration has begun to try to obscure the reality of low AFDC costs and inadequate benefits by adding up the benefits from all the welfare programs and saying the cost is very large and the combined benefit levels to a family are very high. It is true that the cost of all means-tested programs is several times larger than the cost of just AFDC, but that tells us little. For example, our costliest welfare program is Medicaid, the health insurance program for the poor. Some 72 percent—$25 billion of the $34 billion of Medicaid expenditures in FY 1984—went to elderly or disabled recipients, none of whom were on AFDC and many of whom were white, formerly middle-class parents of currently middle-class sons and daughters. This is not the group most Americans think of when discussing welfare reform and the high cost of benefits. Similarly, in 1984 over half of the food-stamp recipients were not in AFDC households. The total-cost argument is a shell game, with the administration betting that it can move the pea faster than the public eye can follow.

Another shell game is the notion that welfare families have a panoply of other benefits and services beyond AFDC available to them, and that the combination of these benefits lifts them out of poverty. This is true in very few cases:

· Although food stamps are available to families on AFDC (as well as working poor families) the combined value of AFDC and food stamps still does not suffice to lift families out of poverty.

· Fewer than one in every four families on AFDC receives housing assistance.

· Attributing the average cost of Medicaid benefits to every family obscures the reality that some families are sick and others are not—that a minority, mostly aged and disabled, use the large majority of health benefits.

Furthermore, the programs often interact in such ways that gains in one cause losses in another. For example, a poor mother can sometimes get help in paying for child care—if she works, at which point she usually loses AFDC benefits equal to her earned income.

Another set of myths revolves around AFDC and sexuality, promiscuity, and illegitimacy. A generation ago the sociologist Herbert Gans wrote about the benefits the affluent get from stigmatizing the poor: "The defenders of the desirability of hard work, thrift, honesty and monogamy need people who can be accused of being lazy, spendthrift, dishonest and promiscuous to justify these norms . . . [T]he norms . . . are best legitimated by discovering violations."[1] Gans went on to argue that whether the poor actually violate these norms more than anyone else is dubious but in any event is irrelevant to the psychosocial and economic gain the affluent derive from the stereotype. If you doubt this, just substitute the word "black" for the word "poor" in Gans's analysis, and think of the stereotypes whites have clung to through American history.

When Gans was writing a generation ago, the most prevalent myth about welfare mothers and sex and babies probably was that the mothers had more babies to get higher welfare grants. Sometimes reality overcomes myths. The average AFDC family size—1.9 children per family—is essentially the same as the size of the average American family. If another child is born, almost invariably the additional grant is so small that it cannot support that child, much less improve the mother's standard of living. Alabama, for example, pays about $30 per month for an additional child; in Florida, it is $40; in Illinois, $60. At such levels, it is not surprising that mothers on AFDC have only one-fourth the number of babies while they are on welfare as do other women who are not on welfare.

The extra-baby-for-profit myth has slowly dwindled, but the United States apparently cannot function without a myth that links welfare and sexuality. So we have a new myth—one that tells us that the availability of welfare is the cause of earlier teen sexuality and greater teen pregnancy, that welfare benefits and the financial independence they imply are such an attractive package that teenagers have babies, out of wedlock, in order to get assistance.

This new myth does not accord with logic or with the findings of studies in the field. It does not explain the earlier sexuality of middle-class girls for whom there is not the slightest expectation of going on welfare. It does not explain why a huge proportion of teen pregnancies are unintended. It does not accord with the census data showing that the birthrate for unmarried black teens has decreased since 1970 (and that for white teens has increased)—at the same time that the myth has become prevalent. And it does not jibe with the research by Mary Jo Bane and David Ellwood at Harvard, and by William Wilson at the University of Chicago, which, as I mentioned in Chapter 3, indicates that welfare is not to blame for out-of-wedlock births.

In fact, in January 1983 the combined value of AFDC and food-stamp benefits for a family of three in Mississippi was 46 percent of the federal poverty guidelines—lower than any other state. Yet, in that same year, Mississippi ranked second in the country in percentages of all births that were out of wedlock. By contrast, Minnesota, which had the twelfth highest combined benefit value, had the seventh lowest rate of out-of-wedlock births. This underscores what I discussed in Chapter 1: that the failure to form black families is tied more to increasing unemployment and decreasing marriageability among black males than to the availability of welfare benefits.

There is no evidence that availability of welfare benefits affects the decision to have a child, and the evidence indicates that level of benefits does not correlate to out-of-wedlock birth rates. There is, however, some relation between marriage and divorce, on the one hand, and the availability or total absence of welfare, on the other. Research has shown that the availability of welfare may affect whether a mother will marry, or whether the marriage will stay together. In other words, welfare—meaning the existence of a bare subsistence grant independent of the man's income—may make women less likely to enter into bad marriages, or more apt to leave ones that have turned bad. The opening of employment opportunities has had a similar effect for better-educated women with decent jobs. In both cases allowing escape from bad marriages can hardly be condemned as universally undesirable.

More problematic is the effect of existing welfare rules on good marriages, because we often do not give welfare to two-parent families. Under the current AFDC program, regardless of how poor they are, two-parent families with children are ineligible for AFDC assistance in half the states, unless a parent is incapacitated. In these states, children are ineligible for assistance unless their families break up. Sadly, the system seems to encourage family breakup as economic strains overwhelm family stability. Data from states that have eliminated welfare for two-parent families show a dramatic increase in the percentage of families that then join the regular AFDC rolls as single-parent families.

In this one area where we know there is a significant correlation between family formation and welfare, however, the Reagan administration has helped to block the remedy: it has opposed congressional efforts to require states to adopt the two-parent AFDC program. The administration is more interested in purportedly cutting costs than in fixing what needs to be fixed and bolstering the family.

A third major set of myths involves the relation between welfare and work. We are told that welfare discourages work and encourages dependency. In essence, many Americans think that most poor families are on welfare, living well enough so that there is no reason to take a job. One corollary of this myth is our seemingly expanding concept of the underclass. The term is inherently vague. It once used to connote, typically, a small subgroup of the poverty population alienated from or hostile to the larger society, often the very poorest, lacking in coping skills and resources, and, therefore, the most difficult to assist. More recently, however, "underclass" has been used more indiscriminately to refer to all those who live in poverty or rely upon welfare benefits for long periods of time.

The danger in this increasing lack of clarity is that references to the underclass will add nothing to our understanding of poverty, but will erode public confidence in our ability to do something about it. If applied too loosely to all who have remained persistently poor, the term underclass may reinforce the misguided belief that poverty is the product solely or primarily of individual pathology, ignoring the institutional forces in our society which help perpetuate deprivation. By implying that there are major differences in the character of the poor vis-à-vis the nonpoor, the term undermines our confidence and desire to try to help.

Without question, there are Americans with such serious personal afflictions that they exist on the fringes of society and frequently in abject poverty. Without question, some segment of the poverty population also relies heavily upon income transfers for sustained periods, although detailed studies of the AFDC caseload suggest that roughly half of all recipients move off the rolls within two years. The remainder rely upon AFDC benefits for a much longer period of time—most at least six years, and a third for eight years or more. Research by Mary Jo Bane and David Ellwood found dramatic differences in the length of spells among different groups of recipients. Women who become female heads of household by having a child, nonwhites, high-school dropouts, mothers with many children, and those with no previous earnings all had longer spells. For example, Bane and Ellwood estimate that "nonwhite unmarried mothers who dropped out of high school will average 10 years on welfare."[2]

Even these realities do not imply that nothing can be done to attack the problems of poverty in the United States. One of the oldest strategies for resisting social changes is to focus attention on the most intractable aspects of a problem and then to cast them as justifications for inaction, complacency, or resignation.

We must not allow such a diversion from the many important and effective steps we can take to help those who are now left behind by current social and economic policies. The belief that there is a growing underclass may reflect some change in the behavior of some poor people. But it seems more likely that the underclass has "grown" not because the behavior of the poor has changed, but because our definition has broadened to encompass more of, if not all of the poor. The number of poor people has grown, so attaching the label underclass, with its pejorative behavioral connotations, is a way of blaming the poor rather than ourselves for the increasingly dire straits of millions of Americans.

The Behavior of the Poor

Contrary to myth, most poor families in America are trying—against growing odds—to earn the income they need to pull themselves and their children out of poverty. Among adults who are not disabled, elderly, or taking care of young children, more than two-thirds of all heads of poor households worked, either full- or part-time, during all or part of 1984. This included more than half of all single heads of poor households and fully 80 percent of men who head poor households.

For a growing number of Americans, however, working does not mean escaping poverty. Instead, the ranks of the working poor have grown, in significant part as a result of changes in the job market and the declining real value of the minimum wage. In 1979 a parent working full time at the minimum wage earned enough to lift a family of three above the poverty line. In 1986, because the minimum wage has not been adjusted for inflation since January 1981, a full-time minimum-wage job yields a paycheck equal to only 75 percent of the poverty level for a family of three, and 61 percent of the poverty level for a family of four.

The trend toward earnings inadequate to support children and families is shocking. In 1984 more than 11.4 million Americans with hourly wages were paid at such low rates (less than four dollars an hour) that income from a full-time job would be insufficient to bring a family of three out of poverty. In 1979 only

2.8 million workers received such inadequate wages. In other words, from 1979 to 1984 the number of Americans working—and willing to work—at jobs that will not pull even a small family out of poverty quadrupled, at the same time that some political leaders have tried to convince Americans that the poor refuse to work.

High rates of unemployment have contributed to declining wages. In distressed regions, which have not been reached by the current "recovery," joblessness remains massive and frighteningly persistent.

In short, substantial segments of the population have been left behind while the nation pretended it was stimulating the economy by redistributing income upward. Those left behind include millions of Americans assuming responsibility for their own lives, working or seeking work in an effort to become economically self-sufficient, but for whom the economy is not working. Some of them are on welfare. Many are not. These millions are, not incidentally, disproportionately young (in their late teens and twenties) and therefore disproportionately at the age when their families include young children. At the same time that we are redistributing income to the affluent, we are also redistributing it to older workers whose children are grown and have left home, as well as to childless workers.

In any event, the work behavior of the poor shows that the poor, including those who rely upon welfare benefits to meet their needs, overwhelmingly respond to the same choices and motivations as the rest of us. They are not somehow fundamentally different. They are us, with less income, and sometimes less education.

Conservatives in the United States have long held the view that the poor are basically different from the rest of us, and that their problems stem primarily from some alleged lack of motivation or effort. President Reagan has been a forceful spokesman for this point of view, claiming that the American economy offers unbounded opportunities, while questioning the motivation of those unable to earn a decent living. This perspective leads conservative critics of the welfare system to exaggerate the current and potential conflicts between basic income supports and work effort, and to focus social policy on molding the behavior of the poor through coercion.

The evidence on work motivation among the poor clearly suggests that the conservatives are wrong. The great majority of able-bodied Americans who are poor both want to work and do work when they have the opportunity. There is much turnover among the poor. Families move in and out of poverty due to layoffs and hiring, wage increases and decreases, illnesses and recoveries, deaths, births, marriages, divorces—the vicissitudes of life that affect all families. Although one out of every four American children receives AFDC at some point in his or her childhood, only 4 percent of all families receive as much as half of their income from AFDC during the period they are raising their children.

If we begin with the premise that the poor respond to the same motivations and incentives as the rest of us, the potential conflicts between work and welfare become much more manageable. The issues then become economic, not behavioral. Poor Americans are no more likely to work than the rest of us when it is clear that their effort will leave them worse off than before. However, because work is so important to our self-esteem and our hopes for the future, economically and otherwise, the poor, like the rest of us, will work even under difficult circumstances and for marginal gains.

The similarities between poor and nonpoor in the United States argue for a broader perspective on the interrelation between work and welfare, and a broader restructuring of our policies to ensure adequate incomes for all members of society. There is a real link between welfare and work, but it is primarily a matter of dollars and cents, not of remedying some perceived pathology among the poor. Poor parents by and large are not those who have refused because of some character flaw to join the mainstream economic system; rather, they are people who have fallen or been pushed out of or never got a strong foothold in that system.

In the United States our generous impulse to help the less fortunate has always been coupled with a Calvinist admonition that help should only go to the truly "worthy" poor, those who cannot work or are otherwise excused from work in the short or long term. This approach has dominated welfare policy throughout American history. Even AFDC reflects it. By giving AFDC almost exclusively to single-parent, meaning female-headed, families, we were giving it to families with adults who were excused from work—at least for the three decades from 1935 to the mid-1960s during which society rarely wanted women to work. But as our expectations of women changed (and as, not incidentally, a higher proportion of those female-headed poor welfare families became black), we shifted ground and started to impose coercive work requirements and other rules to "correct" the behavior of AFDC mothers.

The change in the nature of the caseload also caused an erosion of support for AFDC, as there occurred a clash with stereotyped notions of the proper role of women. Caseload growth in the 1960s was characterized by significant increases in families experiencing divorce, separation, and desertion; unwed mothers and their children; and minorities. The percentage of widows and orphans in the program decreased significantly, as did sympathy for recipients in many states and communities. The 1967 Social Security amendments included not only provisions to encourage recipients to get jobs and remain employed but also several measures that reacted to the changing caseload. One was a birth-control provision for the purpose of preventing and reducing out-of-wedlock births. The most objectionable provision, never implemented and repealed in 1969, was a freeze on federal matching funds to states for AFDC cases attributable to desertion or illegitimacy. The addition in the 1960s of the option to cover two-parent families also contributed to the demands for broader and more coercive work requirements.

Government Programs since the 1960s:
Some Specific Successes

President Johnson's Great Society initiative was predicated much less on the view of the poor that saw them as ill-motivated, and much more on a recognition that the link between welfare and work was economic, and that it made sense to enhance both welfare and wages. In pursuing his vision, Johnson outlined a two-pronged assault against poverty. First, he proposed to broaden economic opportunity and promote self-sufficiency, by investing in education and job-training and by reducing barriers to advancement posed by discrimination in our economic and political spheres. Second, he coupled this drive to open the doors of opportunity for those capable of self-support with attempts to improve income supports for those unable to work or unable to meet their families' basic needs.

In the years that followed some important victories were achieved for some target groups. Most notable has been the dramatic decline in poverty among the elderly through the enactment of the Medicare and Supplemental Security Income programs and improvements in Social Security. The poverty rate of those aged sixty-five and over plummeted from 35 percent in 1959 to 25 percent in 1970, less than 16 percent in 1980, and 12 percent in 1984.

We made far less progress in improving basic income supports for the nonelderly poor during this period. Enactment of the Food Stamp and Medicaid programs represented important advances that have contributed to the health and nutritional well-being of both the elderly and nonelderly poor. Unfortunately, the cash transfers provided to poor families and children through AFDC rose only modestly between 1965 and 1969, and then actually fell drastically in real terms (adjusting for inflation) during the 1970s. Unlike Social Security and Supplemental Security Income, AFDC was not indexed for inflation. As a result of this and of demographic change, the share of total federal spending for income-transfer programs devoted to the elderly and disabled grew from 70 percent in 1960 to 78 percent in 1980, while the portion of such spending going to the nonaged and nondisabled dwindled from 30 to 22 percent.

The Johnson programs designed to fulfill the promise of greater opportunities for advancement, employment, and eventual self-sufficiency unraveled even more quickly. Federal support for education did grow substantially, but federal funding for manpower development and job-training programs did not. The federal government ventured only sporadically into direct job-creation efforts,

during recessions, but made no lasting commitment to public employment programs as a response to high levels of joblessness within poor and minority communities.

The programs did not unravel because they were flawed. This brings us to another myth: that all of the programs of the Great Society have been an abysmal failure. President Reagan likes to quip that we waged a war on poverty and poverty won. More accurately, we declared war on poverty; sent one-third of an army, one-fifth of a navy, and no air force; and still won some battles, while losing some. In many areas we never mounted a serious assault on deprivation and barriers to opportunity; in others we can document success. Yet the myth of "failed social programs" persists, and that myth is used to justify an assault both on welfare and on programs designed to enhance wages and employability.

But even without an adequate sustained commitment, many federal programs launched as part of the antipoverty effort have worked well. Children who have been enrolled in Head Start make large gains in school and later at work. Investments in compensatory education and higher education helped close gaps between white and black children. The Job Corps has been shown to be successful. Medicaid and food stamps and child nutrition programs have had dramatic positive effects in lowering infant mortality and child malnutrition.

By and large, many Great Society programs did not fail. We just did not put enough into them, for long enough, or with enough oversight to assure targeting, careful implementation and thus success. The experience tells us much about the politics of change—how social innovations come to be labeled as successes or failures. One easy lesson is that if we promise too much and deliver too little, it becomes hard to convince the public of the importance of these efforts or to sustain public support for policies which will reduce poverty and welfare dependency. We have to be clearer about what we can expect from limited programs and more specific in our assessments of what did and did not work, and why. The tougher lessons are why the backlash against both prongs of the Johnson program came so soon and so virulently—after all, it began in 1968 with Wallace and Nixon, not in 1980 with Reagan.

The contrast with programs for the elderly is instructive. Social Security and Medicare are widely supported because they are universal, not means-tested, and therefore reach millions of middle-class Americans. This is possible because we are not conflicted about whether the old should work, and do not worry obsessively about their motivation or about the relation between their benefits and wages, even when prevailing wages are low. We no longer expect the elderly to work—indeed we generally do not want them to work. In the 1930s we decided to ration jobs and give them to younger workers, often those with children, by keeping the elderly out of the work force.

On the other hand, we expect those who are not elderly or disabled to work. This was a premise of the education–job-training–nondiscrimination side of President Johnson's program. But we expected too much success too fast. And we did not do enough to bring about that success because there was much resistance. Some just did not want to spend the money. Others did not understand why everyone cannot lift himself or herself up by his or her own bootstraps—even though few Americans really live out this myth of total self-sufficiency. And, equally fundamental, opening doors to jobs and more adequate earnings was perceived as a direct threat to the hard-won gains of the affluent middle class. The expansion of economic opportunities for poor and minority Americans required fundamental changes in the economy that the majority was unwilling to tolerate.

Public employment programs offering adequate wages threatened the interests of employers who depended on a readily available supply of workers at below-poverty wages. Sometimes they appeared to jeopardize wage gains achieved by organized labor. Affirmative action was seen as restricting the access of white, male, middle-class Americans to attractive jobs in the public and private sectors. Community-action agencies that sought to organize low-income neighborhoods quickly came into conflict with entrenched constituencies seeking to preserve political control.

Among the Great Society's attempts to expand economic opportunity, only the education initiatives enjoyed broad and sustained support during the 1970s, although many still serve only a small proportion of the potentially eligible children. Our targeted investments in elementary and secondary education, as well as in student financial assistance for postsecondary education, did open avenues to advancement and self-sufficiency for substantial numbers of disadvantaged Americans.

In the absence of expanded opportunities for employment at the end of the educational process, however, these efforts have proved woefully inadequate. Young black college graduates still face nearly the same chance of being unemployed as white high-school dropouts. And even among full-time adult workers, black males with college degrees on the average earn no more than white males who dropped out of high school.

We have failed to build an adequate foundation of expanded opportunity which encourages motivation, self-reliance, and hope among those who strive for economic security and self-sufficiency. This undercuts our educational programs as well, for poor and minority youth lose hope that their hard work in school will produce fair results during their adulthood. The failure to establish adequate opportunity results from the shortcomings of the private sector and the shortfall of public effort, not the public efforts that actually were made. Moreover, because income transfers for the poor often are no longer accompanied by real opportunities for meaningful work and self-support, and because we have returned to justifying our failure to keep the poor in the economy by stigmatizing their motivation, our means-tested programs have been increasingly saddled with punitive and arbitrary attempts to coerce able-bodied persons to work at below-subsistence wages.

President Nixon's welfare reform effort, the Family Assistance Plan proposed in 1969, was the first U.S. attempt to establish a minimum income floor for all poor families with children, including the working poor, and to do away with AFDC. It foundered in part because of the fight over its work requirements, with both liberals and conservatives critical of its rules. (In addition, the income levels included in FAP were grossly inadequate. For example, over half the states were already providing higher benefits than the $1,600 a year for a family of four originally proposed.)

President Carter's Better Jobs and Income Program five years later fell victim to perceived budgetary constraints. Carter announced early on that the total federal cost of the program would not exceed current expenditures. This resulted in proposals too modest to reshape the inadequate programs it was replacing.

The Carter proposal did acknowledge for the first time the importance of job-creation strategies in any broader welfare-reform effort. But this achievement was also negated by a refusal to commit the needed resources. The Carter plan would have provided 1.4 million minimum-wage jobs, a number which fell short of the level required, with no fringe benefits or provisions for child care. The Better Jobs and Income Proposal never even came to a vote in the House.

The failure of these efforts was in large part the result of inconsistencies among their goals. They tried to address inadequacies and inequities in current benefits, as well as work disincentives and incentives to dependency and family breakup, while holding down costs and not addressing the basic employment and wage problems of the poor.

The policies of the Reagan administration, with fewer goals, have had fewer inconsistencies. Inadequacies and inequities in the program have not been a concern, and the administration has paid only lip service to concern about family breakup. A primary goal of the federal government in the 1980s has been to provide a ready supply of low-wage labor for employers and to ensure that the welfare system does not offer an alternative to jobs at below-poverty wages.

A policy of undermining wages and wage equivalents has been carried out by freezing the minimum wage, by seeking a sub-minimum wage for young workers, by trying to weaken unions, and by a variety of other devices. Simultaneously the administration has tried to erode welfare so that it would not interfere with even the lowest-paying work. Eligibility and benefits were cut. Food stamps were reduced. The administration dropped all nineteen- and twenty-year-olds and many eighteen-year-olds from AFDC, even if they were still in school, in an attempt to push them into the work force. Fearful that welfare would occasionally still be a possible alternative to work, the Reagan administration sought to expand coercive work programs for welfare recipients, both to counter largely illusory incentives to choose welfare over jobs and to move recipients into the low end of the job market, using welfare policy to help erode wages even further. To the administration, attacking welfare is itself a virtue, but it is apparently seen as doubly virtuous because it exerts downward pressure on wage levels. This two-track policy is in some sense the mirror image of the Johnson policy.

Millions have suffered as a result, and our immediate—and correct—instinct is to restore welfare cuts and raise benefits. There is a limit to how far we can go down this path, however, without dealing with work and wage issues. The administration's view of the tie between welfare and behavior may be wrong, but there is a real link between welfare and work for the poor, just as there are broader links between economic incentives and work habits for everyone. No one argues that welfare and work are unrelated.

Directions for Reform

The fundamental questions cannot be solved by tinkering obsessively with the relation between welfare and work, constantly adjusting welfare programs to coerce "proper behavior" and make sure that no unworthy recipient escapes the fine mesh of the work ethic. The fundamental issue is whether we can move beyond our obsession with the motivation and behavior of the poor—their sexual as well as their work behavior—to examine the economic links between wages and social welfare, to recognize that those links exist for all of us and that we can devise ways that the family and the private sector and the government can interact positively for all families, regardless of income. Our obsession with welfare and the allegedly deviant behavior of the poor serves only to obscure broader social needs, not to illuminate the policy debate. It is very much akin to our country's earlier obsession with race and the allegedly deviant behavior of blacks. It obscures our vision of a better society and better family policy for all.

Considering how to arrive at a real pro-family policy suggests ways that government can be used to support wages and opportunity policies and family cohesion for all, as President Johnson tried to do. The beneficiaries are the welfare poor, the working poor, and moderate and middle-income Americans. Instead of worrying whether poor parents of infants on welfare are sufficiently motivated to work, we should move toward a system of universal availability of maternity and paternity leave and benefits, privately and publicly funded, establishing a consensus that we do not demand that a parent with an infant work, regardless of his or her economic status. This Social-Security-like system would assist parents and children, leave the economy unharmed, and would, like Social Security, help ration the limited supply of jobs. Similarly, would it not be good family policy and good economic policy to increase the flexibility for part-time jobs and to begin once again to reduce the hours in a work week?

When we create such flexible work policies with broad coverage—whether a half-year's leave for a parent of a newborn or a half-time job for the parent of a toddler—we give everyone a needed benefit, do not undercut work incentives over the long term, distribute available jobs better, serve other social purposes, and undercut our obsession with the work behavior of the poor. This is not as unprecedented as it sounds. We have a consensus in this country for such policies with regard not only to the elderly but to the disabled (through Social Security), for the insured unemployed, and for children through the age of about seventeen. (These children's policies are embodied in child labor and compulsory school attendance laws.)

Other countries have such policies as well as an analagous but broader policy—called a universal children's allowance—that allows children, who are exempt from work, to eat as well as go to school, without worrying about undercutting parents' work habits. We need some form of minimum guaranteed income for families or negative income tax or children's allowance that will encourage work and still guarantee all Americans a decent living.

According to a recent study by Kamerman and Kahn, the United States is the only Western industrialized nation that does not offer child allowances.[3] These allowances, typically available to every family with children without regard to income, form the nucleus of family social policy in most western European countries. Most of these countries also give supplementary means-tested welfare benefits to some low-income families; but instead of using welfare as the primary method for assisting poor families, they have focused on alternate means of supplementing income which do not single out and humiliate the poor. Such techniques include not only child allowances but advance child maintenance payments if a parent is absent through separation or divorce. (Under such an arrangement, the government usually provides a basic child-support payment, which may later be reimbursed by the absent parent.) Unemployment assistance and maternity or parental benefits are also common.

In every one of the eight countries studied, single-parent families (both those where the mother worked part-time and those where she did not work at all) were better off financially in relation to their country's average wage than similar families would be in Pennsylvania (whose AFDC levels are in the top third of all U.S. states). Poor American two-parent families studied by Kahn and Kamerman fared almost as badly by comparison to similar families in other countries. But the availability of more generous basic benefits to all families does not discourage parents from working in order to seek further economic, social, and psychic gain. Sweden, with the most generous package of family benefits, also has the highest labor force participation for *all* adults, whether single parents or not, and regardless of gender.

Even with a clear consensus on broader exemptions from work, and even with child allowances, we will still need a welfare program as the ultimate safety net, and still have to deal with the relation between welfare and work—by then, let us hope, in a calmer and less stigmatizing atmosphere. Addressing the problem does not mean simply making changes in the welfare system. An exclusive emphasis there ignores the need for basic investments on the work side, which can help more Americans get jobs and earn a decent wage, and which will make it politically possible to raise welfare to decent levels as well:

· We must resume the task of direct job creation, providing jobs in both public and private sectors for those seeking to support themselves and their families;

- We must raise the minimum wage so that a full-time worker will be able to support a family above the poverty line;

- We must guarantee that low-paid workers can get health insurance for themselves and their dependents through their jobs or otherwise;

- We must have a high quality, affordable child-care system, and help lower-paid workers pay for child care.

We need a substantial federal investment in the effort to create jobs. With nearly eight million Americans actively looking for work but unable to find jobs, as well as many others who would work if adequate jobs were available, the expansion of employment opportunities is the most effective mechanism for raising family incomes and promoting self-sufficiency.

Notwithstanding the political attacks focused on programs providing public service employment during the late 1970s, there remains a host of important national needs (including a deteriorating public works infrastructure, neighborhood revitalization efforts, and a wide range of essential human services) that can and must be met through public sector job creation. It is ironic that the same kind of public work activities denigrated in the 1970s as "make-work" are now being heralded as valuable opportunities in the context of "workfare" programs now operated in many states. In both cases there is evidence that the work performed by participants can be useful and productive. The difference is that public service employment provided a paycheck and a decent wage, while strict "workfare" assignments offer neither the dignity of a job nor the prospect of an immediate escape from poverty.

When we have more people at work, and working for family-supporting wages, we will be able to provide family-supporting welfare and unemployment benefits to those who cannot work or are out of work for a while. And we will be able to do this without agonizing uselessly about how to control the behavior of the poor. There will always be some individuals and families that need help, whether because of personal tragedies and afflictions or cyclical fluctuations in a market economy. The United States could provide them with what some members of Congress sought but did not get when AFDC was enacted in 1935: welfare payments that provide "a reasonable subsistence—compatible with decency and health." And we could even reconcile ourselves to supporting decently that small group of the poor—perhaps a group that we can call the underclass—families with a parent who is physically able to work, but unwilling or unable to do so, by training or acculturation. We could recognize that it is more important to our society that every child has enough to eat than that every parent be forced to work. We could act out an old-fashioned notion—one of those traditional notions of which President Reagan is so fond. It is called compassion.

There is one other necessary reform. Although the poor want to work at decent jobs, many are not well-equipped educationally to participate in the mainstream of the new, high-tech economy. Of course, as recent reports on the alarming illiteracy rate among American adults show, it is not only the poor who need training and education. The need for training of various sorts among the middle class is very common, yet we do not stigmatize it or complain about its cost. The most widespread federally subsidized formal job-training system we have for American adults is called continuing education, and it is something in which lawyers, doctors, executives, middle management, and others continually engage. The federal government has been paying as much as 56 percent of the cost of this job-training program through the tax system. By contrast, the welfare recipient or poor person who needs similar (albeit sometimes more basic) training is stigmatized because of that need and the administration wants to abolish the small federal Work Incentive (WIN) program that supports training for welfare recipients.

The most cost-effective way to promote literacy and adequate basic skills is through investments in prevention. For this reason I want to focus more closely on the special needs of disadvantaged youths. I have already discussed the urgency of early interventions in maternal and infant health, child care, and elementary education. Building upon a good foundation of early childhood development, we must make some critical investments in work and learning for poor and minority teenagers if we are serious about preventing long-term dependency. The evidence is increasingly clear that deficiencies in basic skills and lack of early work experience are a crippling combination for at-risk youth, seriously jeopardizing prospects for employment and eventual self-sufficiency. The official unemployment rate for black teenagers (which includes only those actively seeking work) now exceeds 40 percent—three times the rate for their white counterparts. It is our failure to respond to the unmet needs of adolescents which has contributed so greatly to the growing problems of teen pregnancy and persistent poverty.

At the federal level our record in tackling the severe problem of youth unemployment is particularly dismal. During the Carter administration we finally began to mount a comprehensive youth-employment initiative with the potential to provide both a programmatic and a research base for substantial progress. This effort was brought to an abrupt halt by President Reagan in 1981, and years have passed without any significant federal movement in this crucial area.

Some promising local programs have emerged, however, which suggest new directions for a national youth employment effort— programs such as the Connolly Skills Center in Pittsburgh, the Center for Employment and Training in San Jose, Oakland's East Bay Conservation Corps, and the City Volunteer Corps in New York. The most exciting innovations share a common theme: they combine opportunities for immediate training or work experience with requirements for remedial education to improve the basic academic skills of participating youth. This approach yields more lasting employability gains than work experience alone, while at the same time tapping the motivation of young people and reinforcing their sense of responsibility for their own futures. The programs are adopting lessons learned over two decades about the importance of occupational-skills training, work experience, and remedial education for disadvantaged youth. What is new is the integration of these approaches into a coherent strategy for keeping young people motivated and achieving lasting gains in their employment and earnings.

We need a set of national policies that explicitly supports these combinations of work, learning, training, and community service. We could enhance existing models by establishing a system of youth opportunity accounts, whereby teenagers could earn credits through community service, remedial education, or work-experience activities, and redeem them to cover the costs of participation in occupational training, postsecondary education, or subsidized employment opportunities. Such a system would send a powerful message to our young people that they can, through their own initiatives, open the doors to opportunity and advancement.

It is fair to anticipate that President Reagan's welfare-reform study will adopt none of these approaches. It will be up to us to fight for these necessary reforms. This is a fight we are going to have to win if we are to see our society thrive and grow, economically and ethically. It will be a long fight, but that makes it no less worthwhile. In 1985 CDF achieved, after a ten-year struggle, coverage of all categories of very poor pregnant women in the federal Medicaid program. The struggle for the jobs and welfare strategy I have just outlined may well take another ten years, or more. But we have to lay the base now. In the academic community we need more economists and historians with the commitment and courage to challenge today's conventional wisdom, which says that there is no place in our economy for direct federal job-creation efforts. In this era of inactivity and retrenchment, we need research to fuel our next cycle of experimentation and progress in these critical areas.

And we must *begin* now to build the base for the programs I have described. We learned from the ten-year fight over Medicaid coverage of pregnant women that, even in a time when public opinion does not take kindly to government spending, there are springs of compassion that can be tapped; that in an era of cutbacks, it is possible, even necessary, to pursue a positive agenda for change; and that improvements are incremental, requiring patient and careful advocacy over a long period of time.

What changes do we need today? Most urgently, we must rebuild the youth education, training, and employment process. An entire generation of poor and minority youth are being left out or shut out of the mainstream of American society right now. We must fight any efforts, under the guise of welfare reform and "pro-family" rhetoric, and in reliance on the myths I have described, to slash benefits and compound the suffering of the poor. If the administration tries to return the operation of welfare to the states, we must remember that it is the states which currently set the unconscionably low levels for welfare payments, which average $3.87 per day per recipient. We might also want to remember that before the federal government became involved in welfare, through creation of the AFDC program, state mother's-aid programs helped only one-third of those needing assistance; often they denied aid to mothers who had been deserted by their husbands, as well as unmarried mothers, because they were seen as unfit. Before federal welfare legislation in 1935, most of the families deemed "fit" to receive aid were white and Anglo-Saxon. North Carolina and Florida each had one black family in the state receiving welfare benefits. Many localities paid Mexican, Italian, and Czech families less than they paid Anglo-Saxons.

In addition to fighting cutbacks, we must make significant improvements in AFDC in the short term. First, we must try to reverse the built-in incentive for family breakup inherent in the program. States must be required to provide benefits to two-parent families if the breadwinner is unemployed. But this is not enough. Under current rules governing AFDC for two-parent families, stringent eligibility requirements make it hard for many to qualify. If a family's breadwinner works more than 99 hours a month ($3,980 per year at minimum wage, which is 44 percent of the federal poverty line for a family of three and 31 percent for a family of five), the family is automatically ineligible. Other rules mean that families with no recent attachment to the work force cannot qualify for the program at all. This is particularly damaging to young families for whom recent school attendance, or high unemployment rates often preclude work. For example, if in the last two years a nineteen-year-old father was in school for one year and employed for one year, and then became unemployed, he and his family usually could not get AFDC, even if the current unemployed parent component were in place. And I have just described a *successful* poor young father in today's school and job market. We must give benefits to such families to encourage family formation and feed hungry children. These gaps in the AFDC two-parent program must be closed if it is to be really useful.

Second, there is an urgent need to improve the adequacy of welfare benefits. Welfare grants, in real dollars, increasingly fall short of federal poverty guidelines that establish what a family needs for even bare-bones subsistence. States are free to set their own guidelines for financial eligibility and for the amount of welfare they will give. The failure to require any minimum national benefit level has meant that poor children too often have been at the bottom of the state political barrel. The degree to which children's most basic needs for food, clothing, and shelter are met fluctuates widely, depending on where in the country they happen to live. In January 1986 a family with a mother and two children received AFDC benefits equal to $6.48 a day in Kentucky, and $19.17 a day in Vermont.

Even a modest beginning agenda of welfare improvements must address inadequate AFDC benefits. As part of a movement toward a minimum and more adequate—though not sufficient—national benefit level for AFDC families, CDF proposes:

· Giving states incentives to raise AFDC benefits by offering a higher federal matching rate to those that do increase benefits;

· Requiring states, by October 1, 1988, to update their state eligibility (needs) standards to reflect changes in living costs since 1969, the last time Congress required such an adjustment. The standard is a state-set figure that purports to represent, but rarely does, the amount of money families need for reasonable subsistence. Benefit levels may be, and frequently are, lower than the standard of need;

· Setting a national minimum benefit, effective October 1, 1989, that would require that the combined value of AFDC and food stamp benefits equal at least 75 percent of the federal poverty level. While such a benefit level is itself clearly inadequate, it would be a politically achievable, important first step, and states would be given incentives to continue to raise benefits further.

Third, we must restore positive incentives in the AFDC program for parents to work. Before 1981, a working parent whose earned income was low enough could still get an AFDC supplement. Each month, in calculating his or her grant level, the parent was able to shelter, or disregard from earned income, a little more than one-third of earned income—an incentive to obtain and keep work.

In 1981 Congress passed and President Reagan signed a law that virtually eliminated the work-incentive disregard (and capped the work-related expenses that could be offset against income). The administration and its supply-side theoreticians tell us that a 50 percent tax rate discourages work by the rich. Yet they have imposed on AFDC families an effective tax rate that is typically 100 percent, and often exceeds 100 percent, since each dollar of earnings causes a loss of a dollar or more of assistance because of AFDC grant reductions, possible Medicaid, food-stamp, child-care and housing-assistance reductions, and federal taxes imposed on the poor.

These and related changes have been devastating to the working poor. One and a half to two years after the cuts, 80 percent of the hundreds of thousands who lost AFDC benefits in 1981 were still below the poverty line. For many, loss of AFDC also meant loss of Medicaid. Yet in the low-paying jobs that many of these former recipients have, health insurance, particularly family coverage, is usually not available.

To reverse this damage we must raise the minimum wage and restore the work incentives destroyed in 1981. And we must provide for a system of adequate ancillary supports for families in transition from AFDC to self-support. Even families able to earn enough to leave AFDC are economically vulnerable and need continuing assistance with child care and medical coverage and tax relief. Without such assistance, earning a little more than the AFDC grant provides wreaks havoc when AFDC, Medicaid, and child-care supports are simultaneously pulled out from under the family.

In addition to restoring work incentives, we must improve training and employment opportunities for those who want to make the transition from welfare to work. It is clear that the core of any welfare reform strategy must be work. This does not mean just putting recipients in make-work, temporary jobs. Any effective program to help more AFDC recipients achieve the transition from welfare to work must respond realistically to their employment potential, their needs, and the realities of their living situations.

Based on the most recent available data, 60 percent of all adults in AFDC families have not graduated from high school, sharply diminishing their job prospects, and at least one in four has no prior work experience. An Educational Testing Service study in 1983 found that, among AFDC recipients required to register for the WIN training and work placement program, three in five had math skills and nearly half had reading skills below the eighth- or ninth-grade level. Moreover, if AFDC mothers with young children are to participate in work programs, adequate child care must be provided; 61 percent of AFDC parents in 1983 had children younger than six.

A substantial segment of the AFDC population does have the potential to move from welfare to work and eventual self-sufficiency. But these recipients can do so only if they are given adequate help through training and employment programs, transitional child care, and health insurance assistance.

The most effective welfare-to-work programs make intensive investments in vocational training, remedial education, and supervised work experience for AFDC recipients. Good programs, such as those now under way in Massachusetts, Maryland, and Maine, include individualized assessments of participants' employment needs and remove potential barriers to employment by providing adequate child care and other supportive services. They have focused on volunteers from the AFDC rolls—of which there is no shortage—rather than relying on forced-work strategies. Finally, they have attempted to place AFDC parents in jobs that will pay more than the minimum wage, at least after some reasonable period of time, to improve their chances for eventual self-sufficiency.

These programs reaffirm what we should have known all along: that creative approaches to employment and training and meeting health and child-care needs can help families achieve new levels of self-support and dignity. Drawing from them, we can outline a national agenda for education and training of parents on AFDC that focuses on voluntary, rewarding participation rather than on punitive efforts to place recipients in dead-end workfare jobs for no pay.

The challenges ahead are great as we attempt to design a reform agenda to overcome the tensions I have described and put in place a system of supports for families and individuals that ensures an adequate living standard for all of them, regardless of where they reside or the cause of their need, or the number of parents in the home. That system must respect the importance of the family and provide the supports necessary to preserve it; and it must provide employment training and job opportunities, at decent wages, with sufficient support services.

Every gun that is made, every warship
launched, every rocket fired signifies . . . a
theft from those who hunger and are not fed,
those who are cold and are not clothed. This
world in arms is not spending money alone. It is
spending the sweat of its laborers, the genius of
its scientists, the hope of its children.

—Dwight David Eisenhower,
April 16, 1953

5 · Leadership and Social Change

We are living today in a world that permits forty thousand children
to die quite legally each day from malnutrition and infection. On
each of these days nations of the world, led by our own, spend
$2.7 billion—$1,000 billion each year—on weapons of death that
are of no use to the hungry and sick children of the world.[1]

Our political leaders are turning this nation's plowshares into
swords and bringing good news to the rich at the expense of the
poor. An escalating arms race and nuclear proliferation hold hos-
tage the future that we hold in trust for our children; they also
steal the present from millions of the world's children, whose
principal daily enemy is relentless poverty and the hunger and
disease it breeds.

These horrors occur in Asia, in Latin America, in Africa—in
developing countries where, we are inured to believe, life is
cheap, resources scarce, and political leadership weak. But these
horrors also occur in New York, in Los Angeles, and in Boston. In

the affluent America of the mid-1980s, poverty takes one American child's life every fifty-three minutes.* A black baby born in Chicago today is less likely to live to his or her first birthday than a child born in Cuba or Costa Rica. Should we conclude that in the United States life is cheap and resources scarce or that our leadership is weak and corrupt?

In the face of the highest child poverty rate in twenty years, our present administration has targeted poor children and families again, for $6 billion in new budget cuts in Fiscal Year 1987, on top of $10 billion in previous annual cuts in preventive and survival programs for poor children and families since 1980. As if this were not enough, Gramm-Rudman-Hollings threatens to lop off, indiscriminately, hundreds of millions of dollars more at a time of rising child abuse, homelessness, and hunger. This morally bankrupt law seeks mindlessly to lower a $200 billion annual deficit, which sick and hungry children did not cause and which we cannot solve by hurting them.

The Defense Department and programs for children are supposed to suffer roughly equal percentage cuts under Gramm-Rudman-Hollings, although defense spending has more than doubled since 1980, while spending for children and families has shrunk dramatically. Cutting both by similar percentages is equivalent to putting an overweight adult and a malnourished child on the same diet. Contrary to popular perception that Gramm-Rudman-Hollings protects the poor, only ten of more than fifty low-income programs are protected from its budget buzz saw. Even existing commitments to small Head Start children are not protected. Gramm-Rudman-Hollings' across-the-board cuts, far from being "fair," will only exacerbate the existing unfairness of Reagan budget policies. The large corporation that has been paying little or no federal income taxes, thereby contributing billions to the national debt, will be left untouched. So will the wealthy taxpayer who has

*A Maine Department of Human Services study in 1983 found that poor children in the United States die at three times the rate of nonpoor children. This is a conservative study because of the small number of minority children in that state; nevertheless, Maine officials estimated that poverty was the ultimate cause of death of 10,000 to 11,000 American children annually. Ten thousand deaths per year means that there are 1.14 deaths per hour, or one death every 52 minutes and 31 seconds.

been using loopholes to reduce his federal income tax rate to 3 or 5 percent (while families with incomes at the poverty level have been losing 11 to 12 percent in federal income and Social Security taxes).

At the same time, the Reagan administration sought a $34 billion increase in defense spending in FY 1987, on top of $142 billion in defense increases since 1980, in order to make American children more "secure" from external enemies. Even if defense were held to a no-increase beyond a cost of living position, the defense budget would go up another $12 billion next fiscal year—more than the entire national expenditure on AFDC, which many decry as so costly.

How can we make our political leaders understand that American children also need defense against the enemies within? How do we get them to pause, think, and weigh the relative national security interest of investing in a dubious new multibillion-dollar "Star Wars" system to make our defenses impenetrable against enemy missiles or investing in a smaller achievable war against child poverty—a war that saves and enhances rather than threatens human life?

Every poor American child could have been lifted out of poverty in 1986 for less than half the administration's proposed defense spending for FY 1987 alone. The "Star Wars" start-up research costs alone could have lifted 2.5 million children out of poverty in 1986. (SDI equaled $3.5 billion in FY 1986.)

How long will it take us to convince the American public and policymakers that American babies need defense against preventable infant mortality and birth defects? For two consecutive years the improvement in our national infant mortality rates—already a sad fifteenth in the world—has stalled. The national death rate for black infants between one month and one year of age actually increased by 6 percent between 1983 and 1984. If black and white infant mortality rates were equal, about 5,500 black babies would not have died in 1983.

Between now and 1990, 16,500 American babies will die primarily because of low birth weight. We can prevent at least one in nine of these infant deaths and thousands of handicapping conditions simply by providing their mothers with cost effective prenatal care. In 1983 one baby a day might have lived if its mother had received prenatal care. Prenatal care will not only save children's lives, it will save public dollars: it costs $600 to provide a pregnant woman comprehensive prenatal care for nine months; it costs $1,000 a day to try to save a premature baby through neonatal intensive care. For nine days of the Department of Defense's proposed real spending increase, over and above its cost of living increase in FY 1987, every uninsured poor mother and baby could be provided Medicaid, and thus prenatal care, coverage.[2] CDF asked Congress to take steps in FY 1987, aimed toward this goal, but the national administration opposed this—and sought to cut Medicaid again by another $1.2 billion. How many four-pound babies will it take to balance the federal budget?

At a time when UNICEF is mounting a worldwide campaign to immunize children in third-world countries, tens of thousands of American preschool children still need defense against preventable diseases. Our nation plans to build 17,000 additional nuclear weapons over this decade at an estimated cost of $71 billion. Because use of these weapons would destroy life on earth, we have enough to last the entire duration of human life on this planet. By contrast, the Reagan administration budget allowed for only a single month's stockpile of vaccination serum, which would have left two million fewer children immunized against diptheria, pertussis, and tetanus (DPT) at a time when half of all black preschool children are not fully immunized against DPT and polio. Our third national stockpile—of food—is far more massive than our stockpile of serums. We simply refuse to use it to feed children who go to bed hungry every night.

Like most Americans, I support a strong defense and well-defined national security goals. But I also believe that American children need to be made secure from increasing child abuse. An estimated 1.5 million children were reported abused and neglected in 1983, an increase of 200,000 children over the previous year. American children also need defense against growing homelessness, a symptom of the deeper problems of joblessness and a housing market that is squeezing out low- and moderate-income families. A 1984 Department of Housing and Urban Development (HUD) study said that 22 percent of the homeless living in shelters, not including runaway shelters, are under eighteen years old. Over 66,000 children are currently without adequate, permanent shelter. But rather than seeking to provide decent housing and minimal income supports to help families weather unemployment and loss of shelter, our national leaders are emasculating low-income housing programs, cutting millions more from the tattered survival net of AFDC, and providing not a penny of new money for jobs for unemployed families. AFDC recipients, 66 percent of whom are children, get an average daily benefit of $3.87. Federal AFDC funds have been cut $1.7 billion since 1980.

How do we get our nation to defend our children against sickness, against hunger, against homelessness, against too-early parenting, which locks new generations of children and women into poverty and threatens the very fabric of family life?

The Weasels in our Public Life

Sojourner Truth, an illiterate slave woman, had a knack for stating big truths simply. She said: "Now I hear talk about the Constitution and the rights of man. I comes up and I takes hold of this Constitution. It looks mighty big, and I feels for my rights, but there aren't any there. Then I say, 'God, what ails this Constitution?' And you know what He says to me? God says, 'Sojourner, there is a little weasel in it.' "[3]

Well, there are some big weasels gnawing away at the rights of our children and the moral underpinnings of our democratic society. We must identify and fight these weasels if we are to redirect national priorities and achieve the necessary investment in poor children and economic security for poor families in the 1980s and 1990s. The first is the *greedy military weasel* that never can seem to get enough. It currently spends $780 million a day, $33 million an hour, $540,000 a minute. Between 1986 and 1991, at the current rate, this weasel will spend at least another $1.5 trillion. If I had spent $2 million a day every day since Christ was born, I would have spent less than our national leaders want us to believe the Pentagon can spend efficiently over the next five years.

Just a minute's worth of the military weasel's feast would pay for 14,000 monthly food packages to feed pregnant women and infants (through the Supplemental Food Program for Women, Infants, and Children). Seven days worth would fund Head Start for every eligible child, rather than the 16 percent we serve now.

Everything labeled a national security need is not related to national security. The House Armed Services Committee in 1985 found tens of millions of dollars in questionable "overhead" expenses charged to the Pentagon by only seven of the major defense contractors. Here are just a few of them, and the more productive uses to which we could put the taxpayers' money. With the $10,713 for operating losses at a defense contractor's barbershop reserved for senior executives, we could provide 18,800 breakfasts in day-care homes for children of low-income working parents—a program President Reagan proposed to cut more than 37.5 percent in FY 1987. With the $162,149 for giveaways by one firm that included 2,100 necklaces, 500 cigarette lighters, 200 pewter belt buckles, and 25,000 tie tacks (though only 511 ties!), we can provide summer jobs for more than 200 low-income youths—a program the Reagan administration proposed to cut by 35.6 percent in FY 1987. With the $950,698 billed by another firm for the expense of sending staff to the Paris Air Show, we could send 380 more children to Head Start—a program the President proposed to cut by more than $12 million in FY 1987.

Continuously calling the attention of the American public to trade-offs between excessive defense spending and necessary programs for poor children has not yet succeeded in redirecting profligate military spending in any substantial way. We are, however, engaged in the long process of educating more citizens about their choices and shaming more politicians into leaving children's food and survival health care alone. Politicians have not shared with the American people the fact that FY 1987's proposed military budget *increase alone* exceeds *total* federal spending for two of the largest federal programs for the poor, Food Stamps and AFDC, *combined,* for each of the next five years. Yet these programs are repeatedly attacked by the same administration that continues to have taxpayers fund Pentagon waste and the excesses of some defense contractors.

It is important for citizens to struggle to understand and work to demystify a military budget that has for too long been solely the province of the military-industrial complex, selected experts, and political leaders. A growing, informed, and persistent citizen voice demanding more carefully defined national security goals and a balancing of critical internal and external needs is the only way to force American political leaders to make intelligent budget choices over the long run. We must break with our purchase of Armageddon by reflex.

Santayana defined a fanatic as one who redoubles his efforts after he has forgotten his goal. We must curb the fanatical military weasel and keep it in balance with competing national needs before, in President Eisenhower's words, it "threatens to destroy from within what we are seeking to protect from without."

The second threat to our social equilibrium and future is the *unfairness weasel*. Not only have the poor been sent to the front lines of a federal budget deficit reduction war that few other groups were drafted to fight, they have seen their inadequate wages eaten away by inflation and by skyrocketing federal taxes, which increased by 58 percent between 1980 and 1982 alone. Although more than 42 percent of the 13 million poor children lived in families with incomes below 50 percent of the poverty line in 1983, the richest families—the top tenth—enjoyed an average of $5,000 more income after inflation in 1984 than in 1980. While 2.1 million members of families with earned incomes a little above the poverty line were taxed back into poverty by the federal government, scores of huge corporations paid not a dime in federal income tax.[4] No standard of fairness can justify such outcomes in a democratic society.

The two weasels described are the children of a third, which is eating away at our democratic foundation: the *bystander weasel*. Albert Einstein believed the world to be in greater peril from those who tolerate evil than from those who commit it. Democracy is not a spectator sport. I worry about people who opt out of political, bureaucratic, and community processes, even while I recognize that those processes are sometimes discouraging. I worry about men and women who refuse to take a position because of the complexity or controversy that often surrounds issues of life and death. I hold no brief for those who are content to kibitz intellectually about the life choices of millions of poor children without seeing the hunger and suffering behind the cold statistics, or for those who hide behind professional neutrality and shift responsibility for hard societal problems on to others—problems that must be shared if they are to be solved.

Feeding a hungry child or preventing needless infant deaths in a decent, rich society should not require detailed policy analysis or quantifiable outcome goals or endless commissions. They require compassionate action. By all means let us have more careful definition and justification for our policy goals and spending. Let us apply the same cost-benefit standards consistently to the military and to programs for the nonpoor. But let us be careful not to hide behind cost-benefit analyses when human survival is at issue.

Each of us must reflect hard within ourselves, our families, our churches, synagogues, universities, and home communities, about the national ideals we want America to hold. Each of us must then try, "by little and by little," as Dorothy Day recognized,[5] to live them and be moved to act in the personal arena through greater service to those around us who are more needy, and in the political arena to ensure a more just society. One without the other is not enough to transform the United States.

This brings us to the *ineffectiveness weasel,* which keeps us from trying to make a difference or believing we can make a difference, and thereby deprives our nation of desperately needed moral and political leadership at all levels. I am always surprised by the unrealistically grandiose notions many of us hold about the steps required to overcome problems and to bring about change; by the untapped reservoir of talent paralyzed by despair, lack of confidence, and low aim; by the isolation and lack of networking among the various tiers of leadership needed to foster lasting rather than cosmetic changes in American society; and by the historical illiteracy of many citizens, particularly our young, of a proud past carried on the shoulders of ordinary people who found extraordinary strengths within themselves in their desire to serve others.[6]

Bringing About Social Change

Change requires very hard work that must be sustained by a deep caring about the needs of those who lack a voice in our society and about our national mission in a world plagued by hunger, joblessness, and malnutrition. Sadly, General Omar Bradley is right that "we have grasped the mystery of the atom and rejected the Sermon on the Mount . . . Ours is a world of nuclear giants and ethical infants. We know more about war than we know about peace, more about killing than we know about living."[7]

Robert Kennedy echoed this theme when, during his last campaign, he talked to college students about the need to go beyond our total preoccupation with the economic bottom line, which too often obscures a deeper vision of what is really important. He reminded us that the GNP, though important, "does not include the beauty of our poetry or the strength of our marriages, the intelligence of our public debate or the integrity of our public officials. It allows neither for the justice in our courts, nor for the justness of our dealings with each other. The Gross National Product measures neither our wit nor our courage, neither our wisdom nor our learning, neither our compassion nor our devotion to country. It measures everything, in short, except that which makes life worthwhile."[8]

The first step in bringing about change is caring. But caring is not enough. The second step is trying to see a problem whole and then breaking it into manageable pieces for action. One must proceed step by systematic step to mold and assemble the pieces until the whole is positively affected.

Many of us today are puzzled about how to translate our instincts for decency into positive action.[9] Societies have traditionally acted on their compassionate instincts within the extended family or local community. The structures of modern life require us to apply our decency at the state, national, and international levels as well, a difficult psychological and social transition. The transition has been made more difficult because the government is so complex that people do not understand how its resources are divided, and because they have been told—falsely in many instances—that what they wanted to do did not and could not work.

Without losing sight of the broader vision of lifting every American child out of poverty and ensuring adequate health, child care, and educational opportunity for every child regardless of color or class, it is necessary to struggle constantly to define and package this vision in small, actionable bites. A good children's issue, like any issue, must not only be simple but winnable. Sound goals must be specific, must help build toward a larger effort, should unite and involve rather than divide people, and must have as broad a base of appeal as possible.

Step three in being effective is recognizing that effecting change is not a one-shot effort. It will require never-ending citizen monitoring to protect children and families against poverty and nuclear disaster. Individuals and groups that care about the poor must fight constantly to translate laws and rights and policies into realities that improve the daily lives of children, families, the poor, elderly, and homeless. Like your own house, the national and community house gets dirty all the time unless someone cleans it up regularly.

At CDF we have found it relatively easy to win a lawsuit or even to get a law passed. We have found it very hard to translate the legal remedy or right into improved, financed services and community awareness and professional support for the children. For example, in 1974, we filed a lawsuit in Mississippi—*Mattie T. v. Holladay*—to establish the right of more than 30,000 handicapped children to attend public schools and to receive appropriate services. Simultaneously, we worked in Washington to help enact the new Education for All Handicapped Children Act (P.L. 94-142) to establish a federal right to education and strengthen our chances of a state and local legal victory. We did win, after several years, a fine decree to ensure appropriate education for handicapped children. But Mississippi school officials then said they did not know how to educate the range of handicapped children they were now required to serve by the courts and the new federal law. They lacked trained teachers. They lacked the resources to do a good job. They were unwilling or unable to do the outreach to inform and encourage parents of excluded children to come to school.

If these legal victories were to become real in the day-to-day lives of children and parents, it was clear we had to devote our energies to the thankless but critically important task of nitty-gritty implementation, technical assistance, and budget oversight. Local and state superintendents of education and state legislators with varying degrees of knowledge and commitment to handicapped education come and go. As soon as you inform or identify one set of actors, they move offstage and another group needs to be monitored. Our state office in Mississippi has spent the last ten years working with a range of parents and school officials to try to make the decree work: working in the legislature for funding; prodding us in Washington to hold onto the federal law that the administration has tried twice to repeal and for five years to cut back in the budget. And there is no end in sight. Parental and advocacy vigilance has had to continue to withstand further administration assaults. Gramm-Rudman does not exempt handicapped education from its guillotine. Happily, Connecticut's Senator Weicker chairs a key appropriation subcommittee and is one of several strong congressional advocates for handicapped education. But the battle continues on this as on every program for poor children, year after year.

Nevertheless, there are great rewards. Some 750,000 handicapped children are now going to school in Mississippi and throughout the United States. Parents are being empowered to speak for their children. Teachers are being trained. And schools now accept their responsibility to educate the handicapped children who were educational pariahs a mere fifteen years ago.

The fourth step in effective leadership for social change is understanding that thorough homework—good fact-finding coupled with good analysis—is essential if good remedies are to follow and if an effective case is to be made for a particular cause. Too many good intentions and causes are wrecked, and victims left unhelped, by fiery rhetoric, political grandstanding, and simplistic remedies that sometimes create more problems than they solve.

Being soft-hearted, as many label those who advocate for greater attention to human needs, does not mean being soft-headed. Advocates for children and the poor must be as prepared to argue our cause for poor children as effectively as those who represent politically stronger but certainly no worthier constituencies. Because children do not vote or lobby or make campaign contributions, our credibility and usefulness rest in significant part on the thoroughness and timeliness and packaging of our information. Good facts alone certainly do not guarantee success, but misleading facts can discredit a leader and cause.

Step five is recognizing that there are no short cuts to curing most of the complex social and economic problems facing the United States today. Solving them requires a long-haul struggle to disaggregate the usual multiple causes of, and to identify the many groups affected by, problems that often present themselves as a single issue. Too many of us like the big splash, the striking initiative, the public speeches, and the meetings. Too few of us are willing to suffer through the inglorious hard work and attention to detail which are the basis of sound policy development and lasting change.

The United States is a place where incremental changes built over time rather than massive upheavals are likely to produce major social reforms. We tend to distrust huge social surprises. Often, as Dorothy Day knew, it is better to take the long rather than short route to the center, developing public opinion and constituencies along the way.[10]

Important social reformers learned this the hard way. National Child Labor legislation took nineteen volumes of investigative reports and countless speeches and testimony by Florence Kelley, Jane Addams, Jacob Riis, and numerous allies over thirty-four years to enact and sustain. It was passed three times in the Congress before it was finally upheld by the courts in 1941. Elizabeth Cady Stanton began her struggle for women's suffrage in 1848. The Nineteenth Amendment was enacted in 1920. Lydia Marvin Child's

"An Appeal in Favor of That Class of Americans called Africans" was published in 1833. It inspired Harriet Beecher Stowe's *Uncle Tom's Cabin* in 1852. Slavery was outlawed in 1865 after a Civil War that took several hundred thousand American lives.

Charles Houston, one of the great unsung American heroes, submitted his legal strategy memorandum for ending constitutional segregation to the NAACP board for approval in 1930.[11] Twenty-four years later the U.S. Supreme Court handed down *Brown v. Board of Education*—a decision he did not live to see. His successor lawyers are now more than three decades into the struggle to implement *Brown* and its progeny, with no end in sight. Three civil rights acts, hundreds of protest marches, and dozens of martyrs later, the nation wavers and debates whether to turn back or move ahead in the centuries-long quest to root out racial discrimination in American society.

Justice is not cheap. Justice is not quick. It is not ever finally achieved. It is a hard, ongoing process in constant need of new commanders and soldiers who fight and win small wars in big battles. William James said it well: "I am done with great things and big things, great institutions and big successes, and I am for those tiny invisible molecular moral forces that work from individual to individual, creeping through the crannies of the world like so many rootlets, or like the capillary oozing of water, yet which, if you give them time, will rend the hardest monuments of man's pride."[12]

The Bible is replete with the images and power of small things which achieve great ends when they are grounded in faith: a mustard seed, a jawbone, a stick, a slingshot, a widow's mite. We must not, in trying to think about how we can make a big difference, ignore the small daily differences we can make which, over time, add up to big differences that we often cannot foresee. Jacob Riis vented his frequent frustrations about the slow pace of change, about how much telling it took to make one city know when it was doing wrong: "However, that was what I was there for. When it didn't seem to help, I would go and look at a stonecutter hammering away at his rock perhaps a hundred times without as much as a crack showing in it. Yet at the hundred and first blow it would split in two, and I knew it was not that blow that did it, but all that had gone before."[13]

It takes even more telling to make a nation know when it is doing wrong and still more telling to point it in the direction of doing right. But that is our challenge and responsibility.

Step six in the process of creating social change is follow-up. Most institutions, public or private, seldom police themselves. Competing interest groups seeking their ear, coupled with natural inertia, almost assure that any one-shot effort to correct a problem will be agreeably ignored. Being a change agent for poor children or for anything, means being a good pest, wearing down those you want to do something. And you have a better chance of getting something done if you are specific, address one problem at a time, outline what the person responsible can and should do, have thought through why it is in their self-interest to do it, do not mind doing the work for them, and, most important, make sure they can take credit for getting it done.

Step seven in the change process is collaboration and coalition building. Lone Rangers strike out more and more in our increasingly complex and interdependent society and world. Few social problems yield to a single strategy, and few constituencies share clearly defined single interests which alleviate the need to reach out and broaden their base for specific change. How much more true is the need for collaboration among the weaker groups of society, those who must seek strength through cooperation with others with like and specific self-interests. Those mutual self-interests vary from issue to issue and militate against seeking permanent or general coalitions. In his 1796 Farewell Address, George Washington warned that in politics there are no permanent friends. There is no general constituency for children in the United States. There is a child care constituency and, within it, many subgroups that do not always see their common interests (pre-school education, Head Start, Title XX social service, handicapped, and so on). There is an education constituency that divides along many lines, depending on class or specific disadvantage (such as poverty or physical, mental, or emotional handicap). It goes on and on in each of CDF's six program areas that seek to cover the whole child. The challenge is to seek constantly the common threads across issue, class, racial, and geographical lines, where overriding issues like budget cuts or federalism or parental involvement emerge, while simultaneously juggling a range of specific issue, nonideological coalitions that are pursuing narrower goals.

It is important for all of us to get out of our ideological boxes and keep our constituency base from eroding by reaching out to new allies whose general politics we may not like, but whose occasional interest might intersect with ours. The key to winning big for children is for us to broaden our appeal and to push into the mainstream issues that have been viewed by many as just poor or black or liberal. We need to stop preaching to the converted and spend more time identifying new converts. Every good advocate resonates with a statement attributed to Abraham Lincoln: "When I am getting ready for an argument, I spend one-third of my time thinking about what I am going to say and two-thirds about what my opponent will say."

The need for collaboration also has an internal dimension: effective leadership requires good teamwork and an organizational infrastructure that can efficiently integrate a broad range of issues and strategies needed to mount the long-term and comprehensive advocacy required to achieve substantial social changes for any group. The ground rules for social change have become more complicated in the 1980s. The struggles of the 1960s and 1970s against blatant denial of legal and political rights for blacks, for example, have evolved into the grayer and harder challenge of defining and implementing substantive policies to lend meaning to legally or theoretically pronounced opportunities. For example, thousands of middle-class black youths were poised to walk through the doors of opportunity that *Brown* and the Civil Rights Acts of the 1960s opened. I was able to graduate from poor segregated schools in a small South Carolina town and go on to Yale Law School by way of a black college in Atlanta. This college, Spelman, reinforced the strong family and community values of my early years and exposed me and my classmates to black role models with a mission—Benjamin Mays, Martin Luther King, Jr., and Whitney Young—who not only constantly reminded black youth that we could make it, but indeed, that we had a responsibility to achieve and share that achievement with the less-fortunate black community with whom we shared neighborhoods, churches, and classrooms. What we lacked in skills we made up for in will. The hostility of the outside world which told black children we were not worth much was buffered and countered by our families, schools, churches, and mentors who affirmed our worth and worked with us to change America so that we could enjoy the opportunity denied previous generations of black children. In sum, strong families, strong community institutions, shared dreams, and shared struggle both provoked and capitalized on the tide of change which swept the nation in the 1950s, 1960s, and early 1970s.

Today the black community is much more diverse and dispersed. We do not all live in the same segregated neighborhoods, go to the same segregated schools, and meet in church on Sunday. Many role models for poor black youth have moved to the suburbs. Black leadership is similarly dispersed. Unlike the old days, when Walter White and W. E. B. Du Bois and Roy Wilkins lived in the same apartment building on Edgecombe Avenue in Harlem, black leaders don't all know each other any more. This is both good and bad news. Not too long ago, *Crisis* magazine used to list every black college graduate—a task happily now too large to be undertaken. Similarly, black leadership is no longer just the NAACP and Urban League, Operation Push or the Southern Christian Leadership Conference. It is also the heads of the YWCA, the National Council of Social Workers, the American Library Association, the National Council of Churches, the staff of the Methodist Women, and Church Women United. It is the president of the Ford Foundation, and of the State University of New York as well as of Spelman College and Meharry Medical School. It is the mayor of New Orleans or Atlanta, and chairman of the Budget Committee of the House of Representatives, and the Health Commissioner of Massachusetts. It is a general counsel of General Motors and a vice-president at Lazard Freres. The challenge now is to reconnect black leadership links and force a strong, collaborative chain of black leadership in the 1980s and 1990s to address the new challenges of the black community, of which the black family crisis is one symptom. In sum, the task is to hook up Dr. Du Bois's talented tenth with each other and with the masses from whom it has become more distant, thanks to the opportunities which opened up in the 1960s and 1970s.

How do we do this without constricting the choices for black professionals—a problem white professionals never had to confront? Looking back and trying to bring others along adds an enormous burden to middle-class black Americans still trying to get ahead and compete with white professionals who have their own head start.

When I am asked about the state of black community leadership and cohesion today, I answer that it is emerging and struggling to make the transition from procedural to substantive civil rights and to acquire and apply the new tools of advocacy required in this new era (just as many white leaders are). It is obvious that continuing exclusive emphasis on legal and political rights cannot provide the food, child care, quality education, and jobs to bolster healthy family formation. A clear division of leadership function—with some minding the legal and political foundations—must be complemented by leaders and organizations addressing the range of substantive needs of lower-income blacks, and by others skilled in budget analysis and monitoring and manipulating the bureaucracy. These leaders must pay more attention to management and budget realities; to tax, defense, and fiscal policies; to technical data systems and bureaucratic processes; and to more effective use of the media to define the more complex ongoing struggle for social justice. They must also build internal organizational capacities to implement long-term changes and supplement and bolster the traditional charismatic leader.

Step eight in producing social change is understanding that you cannot beat something with nothing. Those who tear down are a dime a dozen; those who build are scarce. It is important to have leaders with vision and who can say what is right rather than just what is wrong. Many of us become so consumed with gaining power that we forget what we wanted to do with it. Good social-change agents must try not just to point out what is wrong but to offer constructive alternatives for what can be tried instead, constantly adjusting the menu of alternatives to changing needs and politics.

Step nine is risk-taking and not being afraid to lose for things that matter. Failure is just another way to learn how to do something right. We do not need leaders who throw in the towel when things do not go right the first, second, fifth, or even the tenth time, or who pronounce all social programs a failure before they have been given adequate time and resources to work. I shudder to think of our nation's loss if Abraham Lincoln had lacked grit and given in to failure. He was plagued through much of his life by a sense of inadequacy. But he kept trying.

He tried to run a business, which failed, leaving him deep in debt. He was elected to the U.S. House of Representatives in 1846, but was defeated for reelection in 1848 and withdrew from politics. He sought and failed to get a job with the U.S. Land Office. In 1854 he ran for the U.S. Senate and lost. He changed parties and ran again in 1858—and lost again. In 1856 he was talked of as a possible vice-presidential nominee, but it did not come his way. Two years later he was beaten by Stephen A. Douglas. But in 1860 he tried again, and won. And what a profound debt the nation owes him.

The tenth and final step in the change process is confidence and an ability to keep dreaming, to persist, and to avoid low aim. Sojourner Truth, a woman who could neither read nor write, pointed a way for us. She never gave up talking or fighting against slavery and the mistreatment of women, not even against odds far worse than those we and our children face today. Once a northern Ohio man rudely confronted her, asking, "Old woman, do you think that your talk about slavery does any good? Why, I don't care any more for your talk than I do for the bite of a flea." "Perhaps not, but the Lord willing, I'll keep you scratching," Sojourner replied.[14] Every single person can be a flea and can bite. Enough fleas can make even the biggest dog—the biggest institutions— mighty uncomfortable. If they flick some of us off, and others of us keep coming back, we will begin to get the basic human needs of the poor heard and attended to and oil the creaks of our institutions that many say no longer work.

The United States today has the challenge and opportunity of showing the world a living justice by eradicating child poverty and putting a floor of decency under every American family. To do less is to betray our highest ideal. This task cannot be relegated just to government or to somebody else. Every individual has a responsibility to try to make a difference, to give imaginative flesh to the ideal of justice. We should aim high.

Dr. Benjamin E. Mays, the former president of Morehouse College in Atlanta, Georgia, a role model for me and for thousands of other black men and women of my generation, including Martin Luther King, Jr., summed up this quest when he said: "It must be borne in mind that the tragedy of life doesn't lie in not reaching your goal. The tragedy lies in having no goal to reach. It isn't a calamity to die with dreams unfulfilled, but it is a calamity not to dream. It is not a disaster to be unable to capture your ideal, but it is a disaster to have no ideal to capture. It is not a disgrace not to reach the stars, but it is a disgrace to have no stars to reach for. Not failure, but low aim, is sin."[15]

Notes

1. The Black Family in America

1. National Center for Health Statistics, "Induced Terminations of Pregnancy: Reporting States, 1981: Final Data," Monthly Vital Statistics Report, vol. 34, no. 4, supplement (2), United States Public Health Service, Washington, D.C., July 30, 1985, table D, page 4, and calculations by Children's Defense Fund. Unmarried black women who are pregnant are less likely to have abortions than unmarried white women who are pregnant, although the rates among unmarried teenagers are converging. Rates are customarily given per 1,000 women rather than per 1,000 pregnant women, and must be adjusted for the higher pregnancy rates among unmarried black women of all ages.

2. U.S. Bureau of Labor Statistics, unpublished tabulations from the March 1984 Current Population Survey, based on 1983 calendar year income; calculations by CDF.

3. E. Franklin Frazier, *The Negro Family in the United States* (Chicago: University of Chicago Press, 1939, rev. 1969); W. E. B. Dubois, *The Negro American Family* (Atlanta: Atlanta University Press,

1908; Cambridge, Mass., MIT Press, 1970); Daniel Patrick Moynihan, *The Negro Family: The Case for National Action* (Washington, D.C.: U.S. Dept. of Labor, Office of Policy Planning and Research, 1965).

4. Andrew Billingsley, *Black Families in White America* (Englewood Cliffs, N.J.: Prentice-Hall, 1968); Robert B. Hill, *Strengths of Black Families* (New York: Emerson Hall, 1972). See also Robert B. Hill, *Economic Policies and Black Progress: Myths and Realities* (Washington, D.C.: National Urban League, 1981).

5. Herbert G. Gutman, *The Black Family in Slavery and Freedom, 1750–1925* (New York: Random House, 1976); John W. Blassingame, *The Slave Community* (New York: Oxford University Press, 1979): Eugene Genovese, *Roll Jordan Roll: The World the Slaves Made* (New York: Pantheon, 1974).

6. Jessie Shirley Bernard, *Marriage and Family among Negroes* (Englewood Cliffs, N.J.: Prentice-Hall, 1966). See also Joyce A. Ladner, *Tomorrow's Tomorrow* (Garden City, N.Y.: Doubleday, 1971); Robert Staples, ed., *The Black Family: Essays and Studies* (Belmont, Calif.: Wadsworth, 1978); Walter R. Allen, "The Search for Applicable Theories of Black Family Life," *Journal of Marriage and the Family*, 40 (February 1978): 117–129; Robert Staples, "Toward a Sociology of the Black Family: A Decade of Theory and Research," *Journal of Marriage and the Family*, 33 (February 1971): 19–38; William G. Harris, "Research on the Black Family: Mainstream and Dissenting Perspectives," *Journal of Ethnic Studies*, 6 (Winter 1979): 45–64.

7. Harriette Pipes McAdoo, *Black Families* (Beverly Hills, Calif.: Sage, 1981); Eleanor Engram, *Science, Myth, Reality: The Black Family in One-Half Century of Research* (Westport, Conn.: Greenwood, 1982). See also John Reid, *Black America in the 1980s*, Population Reference Bureau, Population Bulletin, 37, no. 4 (December 1982).

8. U.S. Bureau of the Census, Current Population Reports, series P-20, no. 399, "Marital Status and Living Arrangements, March 1984" (Washington, D.C.: Government Printing Office, 1985), and previous annual editions. Since 1950 the Census Bureau also has published a subject report, "Marital Status," as part of volume 2 of each decennial census. Because the current population survey begins in the late 1960s, longer-term comparisons are taken from the decennial census subject reports.

9. The undercount of the population is a matter that has been long investigated by the Bureau of the Census. It is established by comparing the counts taken during the Census with many alternative sources: vital statistics, administrative records, special intensive campaigns to locate persons missed, and smaller random surveys that employ better meth-

ods and more skilled interviewers than are used in the full census. The most reliable alternative is the vital statistics system. Birth and death reporting in the United States is essentially complete. The sex ratio at birth is almost exactly equal; a tiny excess of male over female births is reduced by a slightly greater death rate among male infants in the first year of life.

Deaths are accurately reported and, given the higher rates of male deaths over female deaths, available by five-year age groups for each sex within each race. One can then compare the theoretical sex ratio among twenty- to twenty-five-year-old blacks to that actually found in the Census reports, and observe how that comparison has changed over the decades. The conclusion—that there was no increase in the young black male undercount to explain the decline in young black family formation during the 1970s—is consistent with the Census Bureau's own internal studies. The most recent published review is: U.S. Bureau of the Census, Current Population Reports, series P-23, no. 115, "Coverage of the National Population in the 1980 Census, by Age, Sex, and Race: Preliminary Estimates by Demographic Analysis" (Washington, D.C.: Government Printing Office, 1982).

10. William J. Wilson, remarks at Children's Defense Fund National Conference, February 1986, as a panelist in a session entitled "Teen Pregnancy and Welfare: Part of the Problem or Part of the Solution"; see also William J. Wilson, "Poverty and Family Structure: The Widening Gap between Evidence and Public Policy Issues" (unpublished paper, February 1985).

11. Sarah Bradford, *Harriet Tubman: The Moses of Her People* (New York: Corinth Books, 1986, reprint 1961 ed.); and Gerda Lerner, *Black Women in White America: A Documentary History* (New York: Vintage, 1973).

12. Russell L. Adams, *Great Negroes, Past and Present* (Chicago: Afro-Am Publishing, 1984) p. 26; Rayford W. Logan and Michael R. Winston, eds. *Dictionary of American Negro Biography* (New York and London: W. W. Norton, 1982), pp. 278–280.

13. Logan and Winston, eds., *Dictionary of American Negro Biography*, pp. 12–13.

14. Ibid., pp. 602–603.

15. Adams, *Great Negroes, Past and Present*, p. 109.

16. Ibid., p. 121

17. Lerner, *Black Women in White America*, pp. 134–143.

18. Genna Rae McNeil, *Groundwork: Charles Hamilton Houston and the Struggle for Civil Rights* (Philadelphia: University of Pennsylvania Press, 1983).

19. Martin Luther King, Jr., *Where Do We Go From Here: Chaos or Community?* (Boston: Beacon, 1968), p. 109.

2. The American Family in the 1980s

1. David Broder, "Phil Gramm's Free Enterprise," *The Washington Post,* February 16, 1983; Steven V. Roberts, "Phil Gramm's Crusade Against the Deficit," *New York Times* Magazine, March 30, 1986, p. 21. Roberts said of Gramm: "His tuition in graduate school was paid in part by a National Defense Education Act Fellowship, a possible source of embarrassment now that his legislation is causing the loss of 90,000 federally funded scholarships" (p. 40). Jacqueline Cames, "Gramm: Making Waves, Enemies and History," *Congressional Quarterly,* March 15, 1986, pp. 611–615.

2. Meir, Canticles Rabbah (Midrash) 1.4.; in Joseph L. Baron, ed., *A Treasury of Jewish Quotations* (New York: Aronson, 1985), p. 48.

3. Wiliam S. Nersesian, M.D., Michael R. Petit, M.S.W., Ruth Shaper, M.A., Don Lenieux, M.B.A., and Ellen Naor, M.S., "Childhood Death and Poverty: A Study of All Childhood Deaths in Maine, 1976 to 1980," *Pediatrics,* 75 (January 1985): 41, and Maine Department of Human Services, "Children's Deaths in Maine: 1976-1980 Final Report" (Bangor, Me., April 1983).

4. "Society must act on the highest principles, or its punishment incessantly comes within itself. The neglect of the poor, and tempted, and criminal is fearfully repaid." Charles Loring Brace, *The Dangerous Classes of New York and Twenty Years's Work Among Them* (Montclair, N.J.: Patterson Smith, 1967; repr. of 1880 ed.); quoted in Robert H. Bremner, *From the Depths: The Discovery of Poverty in the United States* (New York: New York University Press, 1956), p. 3.

5. Moore, Thomas, et al., *The Perinatal and Economic Impact of Prenatal Care in a Low Socioeconomic Population,* (San Diego: University of California, San Diego, 1985). The cost is $5,168 per mother and child without public prenatal care and $2,974 per pair with it, both averaged over the low-income population as a whole and counting only costs in the first year after birth. National Academy of Sciences, Institute of Medicine, *Preventing Low Birthweight* (Washington, D.C., 1985). Every dollar spent to provide comprehensive prenatal care could save $3.38 in the first year of life, all probabilities weighted. Michigan Department of Public Health, *Prenatal Care: A Healthy Beginning for Michigan's Children* (Lansing, Mich., 1984). Every dollar spent on prenatal care among low-income women saved $6.12, derived from a 25 percent reduction in the occurrence of low birth weight alone.

6. "Opportunities for Success: Cost Effective Programs for Children,"

Staff Report, House Select Committee on Children, Youth, and Families, August 14, 1985.

7. Bremner, *From the Depths*. See also Robert H. Bremner, et al., eds., *Children and Youth in America: A Documentary History*, vol. 1, 1600–1865, and vol. 2, 1866–1932 (Cambridge, Mass.: Harvard University Press, 1970 and 1971).

3. Preventing Adolescent Pregnancy

1. For teen pregnancy data by race, age, and state, see the following CDF publications: *Maternal and Child Health Data Book: The Health of America's Children* (1986); "Preventing Children Having Children: What You Can Do" (1985); "Adolescent Pregnancy: Whose Problem Is It?" (1986).

2. Elise Jones et al., "Teenage Pregnancy in Developed Countries: Determinants and Policy Implications," *Family Planning Perspectives*, 17, no. 2 (March–April 1985).

3. CDF, "Preventing Adolescent Pregnancy: What Schools Can Do" (September 1986).

4. Among never married black women age eighteen to twenty-four the highest number of children ever born per 1,000 women, and the lowest percent childless, are in the South, where the smallest percent of the black population lives in central cities. U.S. Bureau of the Census, Current Population Report, series P-20, no. 401, "Fertility of American Women: June 1984," table 2 (Washington, D.C.: Government Printing Office, 1985). Older data show birth rates among black women aged eighteen to thirty-four in nonmetropolitan areas at 1,689 births to date per 1,000 women, while the comparable rate in central cities was 1,535 births to date per 1,000 women. U.S. Bureau of the Census, Current Population Report, series P-20, no. 387, "Fertility of American Women: June 1982," table 2, (Washington, D.C.: Government Printing Office, 1984).

5. See CDF publications *A Manual on Providing Effective Prenatal Care Programs for Teens* (1985) and "Building Health Programs for Teenagers" (1986).

6. See CDF, *Adolescent Pregnancy Child Watch Manual* (1984) and other publications.

7. In 1986 those topics included: "Adolescent Pregnancy: Whose Problem Is It?"; "Building Health Programs for Teenagers"; "Adolescent Pregnancy: What the States Are Saying"; "Model Programs: Preventing Adolescent Pregnancy and Building Youth Self-Sufficiency"; "The Schools' Role in Preventing Teen Pregnancy"; "Teen Pregnancy and

Welfare." During 1987 topics are expected to include: "Youth in Out of Home Settings: A Special At Risk Group"; "Teen Parents and Child Care"; "Employment and Training for Teens"; "Prenatal Care for Teen Mothers."

8. See chapter 2, "An Agenda for Adolescent Pregnancy Prevention and Youth Self-Sufficiency," pp. 29–51.

9. Mary Jo Bane and William Julius Wilson, remarks at Children's Defense Fund National Conference, February 1986, on a panel entitled "Teen Pregnancy and Welfare: Part of the Problem or Part of the Solution"; Mary Jo Bane and David Ellwood, "Single Mothers and Their Living Arrangements" (unpublished paper, February 1984); William Julius Wilson and Kathryn Neckerman, "Poverty and Family Structure: The Widening Gap between Evidence and Public Policy Issues" (unpublished paper, February 1985).

4. Supporting Families: Jobs and Income

1. Herbert Gans, *More Equality* (New York: Vantage, 1974), p. 108.

2. Mary Jo Bane and David T. Ellwood, "The Dynamics of Dependence: The Routes to Self-Sufficiency" (unpublished paper, June 1983), p. 30.

3. Sheila Kamerman and Alfred Kahn, "Income Maintenance, Wages, and Family Income," *Public Welfare*, Fall 1983, pp. 23–48; see also, by the same authors, *Family Policy, Government and Families in Fourteen Countries* (New York: Columbia University Press, 1978).

5. Leadership and Social Change

1. UNICEF, *State of the World's Children* (New York: Oxford University Press, 1985); United States Arms Control and Disarmament Agency, *World Military Expenditures and Arms Transfers, 1972–1982* (April 1984); Ruth Leger Sivard, *World Military and Social Expenditures* (New York: Public Affairs Committee, 1985). Domestic spending tradeoffs are from CDF's *A Children's Defense Budget: An Analysis of the FY 1987 Federal Budget and Children* (1986), and previous annual analyses of the President's budget and children from 1982 to 1985.

2. CDF, *A Children's Defense Budget.*

3. Victoria Ortiz, *Sojourner Truth, A Self-Made Woman* (Philadelphia and New York: Lippincott, 1974), pp. 67-68. See also Aletha Jane Lindstrom, *Sojourner Truth, Slave, Abolitionist, Fighter for Women's Rights* (New York: Julian Messner, 1981); Helen Stone Peterson, *Sojourner Truth, Fearless Crusader* (Champaign, Ill.: Garrard, 1972); Arthur Huff

Fauset, *Sojourner Truth, God's Faithful Pilgrim* (New York: Russell and Russell, 1938, rev. 1971).

4. CDF, *A Children's Defense Budget,* chap. 8, "Taxes and Poor Families"; CDF, *The Impact of Federal Taxes on Poor Families* (1985); Robert S. McIntyre and Robert Folen, *Corporate Income Taxes in the Reagan Years: A Study of Three Years of Legalized Corporate Tax Avoidance* (Washington, D.C.: Citizens for Tax Justice, 1984).

5. Robert Ellsberg, ed., *By Little and By Little: The Selected Writings of Dorothy Day* (New York: Knopf, 1983).

6. Albert Schweitzer said that "everyone must work to live, but the purpose of life is to serve and to show compassion and the will to help others. Only then have we ourselves become true human beings." Albert Schweitzer, *Thoughts for Our Times,* ed. Erica Anderson (Mount Vernon, N.Y.: Peter Pauper, 1975), p. 49. Einstein agreed that only a life lived for others is a life worthwhile. George Seldes, *The Great Thoughts* (New York: Ballantine, 1985), p. 119.

7. Address, Armistice Day, 1948.

8. Speech, Cheyenne, Wyoming, April 26, 1968.

9. I have profited greatly over the years from reading and talking to a number of wise role models. I particularly recommend by John Gardner, *Self-Renewal* (New York: Harper & Row, 1964), *Excellence* (New York: Harper, 1961), and "The Nature of Leadership," *Leadership Papers* II (January 1986); Saul Alinsky, *Reveille for Radicals* (New York: Vintage, 1969); Dorothy Day, *The Long Loneliness: The Autobiography of Dorothy Day* (New York: Harper & Row, 1981), *Loaves and Fishes* (New York: Harper & Row, 1963), and *By Little and By Little;* Martin Luther King, Jr., *The Strength to Love* (New York: Harper & Row, 1963), and *Why We Can't Wait* (New York: Harper & Row, 1964); James M. Washington, *A Testament of Hope: The Essential Writings of Martin Luther King, Jr.* (San Francisco: Harper & Row, 1986); Leo Tolstoy, *The Kingdom of God is Within You* (New York: Noonday Press, 1961); E. Stanley Jones, *Mahatma Gandhi: An Interpretation* (New York: Abindon-Cokesbury, 1948); Erik Erikson, *Gandhi's Truth: On The Origin of Militant Nonviolence* (New York: W. W. Norton, 1969); and Albert Camus, *The Fall* (New York: Modern Library, 1964).

10. Daniel Berrigan, Introduction to Dorothy Day, *The Long Loneliness,* p. xx.

11. Genna Mae McNeil, *Groundwork: Charles Hamilton Houston and the Struggle for Civil Rights* (Philadelphia: University of Pennsylvania Press, 1983).

12. William James; quoted in Margaret Quigley and Michael Garvey, eds., *The Dorothy Day Book: A Selection from Her Writings and Readings* (Springfield, Ill.: Templegate, 1982), p. 10.

13. Jacob Riis, *The Making of An American;* quoted in Robert H. Bremner, *From the Depths: The Discovery of Poverty in the United States* (New York: New York University Press, 1956), p. 204.

14. Ortiz, *Sojourner Truth, A Self-Made Woman* (Philadelphia and New York: J. B. Lippincott, 1974), p. 67.

15. Benjamin Mays, *Quotable Quotes of Benjamin Mays* (New York: Vintage, 1983), p. 3 of chapter entitled "Life."

Index